Japanese Politics

Decay or Reform?

The Consequences of Political Stagnation
and the Prospects for Major Change

by Frank McNeil

The Carnegie Endowment for International Peace

Copyright© 1993 by the

Carnegie Endowment for International Peace

2400 N Street, N.W., Washington, D. C. 20037

All rights reserved

Design & Production: Wickham & Associates and Studio Services, Inc.
Copy Editor: Stephanie Terry
Cover: Wickham & Associates

McNeil, Frank

ISBN: 0-87003-027-2

The Carnegie Endowment for International Peace

The Carnegie Endowment was founded in 1910 by Andrew Carnegie to promote international peace and understanding. To that end the Endowment conducts programs of research, discussion, publication, and education in international affairs and American foreign policy. The Endowment also publishes the quarterly journal *Foreign Policy*.

As a tax-exempt operating foundation, the Endowment maintains a professional staff of Senior and Resident Associates who bring to their work substantial firsthand experience in foreign affairs. Through writing, public and media appearances, Congressional testimony, participation in conferences, and other activities, the staff engages the major policy issues of the day in ways that reach both expert and general audiences. Accordingly the Endowment seeks to provide a hospitable umbrella under which responsible analysis and debate may be conducted, and it encourages Associates to write and speak freely on the subjects of their work. The Endowment convenes special policy forums and, from time to time, issues reports of commissions or study groups.

The Endowment normally does not take institutional positions on public policy issues. It supports its activities principally from its own resources, supplemented by non-governmental, philanthropic grants.

Officers

Chairman of the Board	Charles J. Zwick
Vice Chairman of the Board	Robert Carswell
President	Morton I. Abramowitz
Secretary	Larry L. Fabian
Director of Finance and Administration	Michael V. O'Hare

Trustees

Morton I. Abramowitz
President, Carnegie Endowment

Charles W. Bailey II
Journalist

Harry G. Barnes, Jr.
Executive Director, Critical Languages and Area Studies Consortium

Douglas J. Bennet, Jr.
President, National Public Radio

Robert Carswell
Partner, Shearman & Sterling

Gregory B. Craig
Partner, Williams & Connolly

Richard A. Debs
*Advisory Director,
Morgan Stanley & Co.*

William H. Donaldson
*Chairman & CEO,
New York Stock Exchange*

Marion R. Fremont-Smith
Partner, Choate, Hall & Stewart

James C. Gaither
*Partner, Cooley, Godward,
Castro, Huddleson & Tatum*

Leslie H. Gelb
New York Times

Shirley M. Hufstedler
Partner, Hufstedler, Kaus & Ettinger

Thomas L. Hughes
*President Emeritus,
Carnegie Endowment*

James A. Johnson
*Chairman of the Board and CEO,
Fannie Mae*

Wilbert J. LeMelle
President, The Phelps-Stokes Fund

Stephen R. Lewis, Jr.
President, Carleton College

George C. Lodge
Professor, Harvard University

Jessica T. Mathews
*Vice President,
World Resources Institute*

Newton N. Minow
Counsel, Sidley & Austin

Barbara W. Newell
*Regents Professor,
Florida State University*

William J. Perry
*Chairman, Technology
Strategies & Alliances*

Wesley W. Posvar
*Former President,
University of Pittsburgh*

Edson W. Spencer
Spencer Associates

Strobe Talbott
*Editor-at-Large,
Time Magazine*

Charles J. Zwick
Retired Chairman, Southeast Banking Corporation

Foreword

In the summer of 1969 I heard a brilliant introduction to Japanese politics from a talented young political officer in the U.S. embassy in Tokyo: Frank McNeil. Since those days, McNeil has served three times as deputy assistant secretary of state, as U.S. ambassador to Costa Rica, and, after retirement, as executive director of the Commission on U.S.-Japan Relations for the Twenty-first Century. In this essay, McNeil, with the benefit of decades of Japan watching topped by recent trips to Japan and interviews with a substantial number of political leaders, reflects on the origins and nature of Japan's political difficulties.

Just as Japan is emerging as the world's dominant economic power, its politics are approaching gridlock. When Japan was weak economically, no one except a handful of Japan specialists would have cared. Now that Japan is a new global superpower, anyone concerned with international affairs needs a deeper understanding of how Japan's domestic politics shapes its world role.

McNeil makes it clear that democracy now has deep roots in Japan. Governmental leaders are chosen in honest elections, individual rights are protected, and the Japanese people are comfortable with democratic institutions. Japan is today in no danger of slipping into a prewar-style military or totalitarian government.

It is the workings of Japanese democracy that are at issue, including defects in the electoral system, popular apathy and disgust with scandals caused by the link between politicians and powerful interest groups, and a powerless prime ministership. In the United States, election districts are adjusted in size automatically after each census as the population shifts from one area to another. In Japan, no such automatic adjustment has taken place. The Japanese Supreme Court has declared that elections will be invalid if the size of population electing a given official varies too greatly, and it is now very difficult for the politicians even to broker an acceptable plan of redistricting. As Japan has grown richer, not only has the scale of political contributions greatly increased, but a class of nouveau riche with little commitment to the common good has increased its leverage over politicians. Furthermore, the opposition parties, though strong enough to force the Liberal Democratic Party to adapt to keep public support, have never gained enough strength to become a serious alternative prepared to take power. And factionalism without strong leaders has made it difficult for any prime minister to achieve consensus on important issues.

How did politics in Japan come to this impasse? What does it mean for Japan's capacity to keep good relations with the United States and other countries? Might Japan go autarkic? How might the political impasse be broken? Those are the issues that McNeil wrestles with in an unusually perceptive, nuanced, and well-informed presentation.

—*Ezra F. Vogel*
Henry Ford II Professor
of the Social Sciences
Harvard University

Preface

This essay draws on wide-ranging conversations over the past three years with national and local politicians and persons from government, media, business, think tanks, and academia as part of research for a book dealing with the much more extensive subject of democracy in Japan, currently in preparation for the Crown Publishing Group. During a spring 1992 trip to Japan sponsored by the Carnegie Endowment for International Peace, I held background interviews and conversations with more than 40 knowledgeable Japanese plus a handful of foreign observers. That information was supplemented with later research, facilitated by the Asia Foundation, on new directions at the grassroots. The assessment of political institutions in earlier years comes from the experience of working in several cities in Japan for nearly ten years during the period 1957–1971, including four years of following politics on a daily basis for the American embassy in Tokyo.

The inquiry greatly benefits from a willingness, over four decades, of Japanese from all walks of life and from all parts of the country to talk about their politics. To sharpen contention, the Carnegie Endowment sponsored a lively discussion, chaired by Ezra Vogel of Harvard University, of an early version of this paper. I owe gratitude to all those, Japanese and American, who contributed ideas; the responsibility for the study, however, is mine alone. The views herein expressed do not represent the views of the Carnegie Endowment or the Commission on U.S.-Japan Relations for the Twenty-first Century, or those of my new employer, the Center for Naval Analysis.

—*Frank McNeil*

Overview

Some key judgments in this study challenge the usual Western discussion of Japan. For many Western commentators, Japan's democracy is disconnected from the great economic concerns of the post–Cold War era. Except for the powerful bureaucracy, political institutions have been treated as largely irrelevant to international behavior—as political archaeology, suitable for specialists but distant from today's challenges. To cite but one example, media coverage of the July 1992 G-7 summit highlighted the constraints of American and European politics on summit decisions about such matters as the impasse in GATT. There was, however, no such discussion of Japan, much less of its coming political crisis.

This paper takes a different view, arguing that politics and the health of Japan's democracy have become matters of vital importance beyond Japan's isles. Many of that nation's difficulties in dealing with domestic and international problems are rooted in its politics. Some of the causes are unique to Japan, but its political troubles also partake of a post–Cold War phenomenon afflicting other democracies, including our own. There is a sense that political institutions in the developed democracies are not responding effectively to domestic needs and new international challenges. In the words of a highly placed Japanese describing the mood at a meeting among Europeans, Americans, and Japanese, "The United States, Western Europe, and Japan had won the Cold War. We should have been celebrating, but no one was celebrating."

It should be said at the outset that Japan is a democracy. Those who say otherwise hold Japan to a standard to which they do not hold established Euro-American democracies. Japan has operating democratic institutions, elections are honestly counted, and individual rights are protected in law—to a great extent, in fact, though their observance is flawed by evident discrimination against minorities. In Japan, as here and in Europe, it is the performance of democratic institutions, not their existence, that deserves critical examination.[1]

Until recently, Japan's democratic institutions, whatever their deficiencies, worked reasonably well. We tend to forget that Japan's democratic transition was one of the most remarkable in history. Democratic institutions made possible Japan's economic miracle and its peaceful approach to international relations, vital factors in the successful containment of the Soviet Union and in the climate of stability that has sheltered economic and political development in the Pacific since the Vietnam War.

While it was the American occupation that instituted democratic reforms, those reforms encountered native roots and expression among Japanese, who were conscious of the lessons of war and the failures of Japan's prewar democratic experiment. For much of the postwar era, political institutions provided choice and change, something not always understood at the time because in election after election the citizenry deliberately chose the ruling Liberal Democratic Party (the LDP) for its economic policies. Democracy became the enabling element for domestic progress.

Today, Japan's political institutions have declined significantly in effectiveness. Their decline is responsible for the corruption that undermines public confidence and for the policy gridlock—for lack of a better phrase—that hampers domestic and international decision making. The decline began in the mid 1970s, when accumulated deficiencies began to weigh down the political system's responsiveness, representativity, and capacity for decision. By the late 1980s, the deficiencies were highly visible: a dysfunctional electoral system for the dominant Lower House in Japan's parliament; a talented, powerful, but increasingly hide-bound central bureaucracy; a ruling LDP in thrall to money and faction; and an "eternal opposition" unready to take power. By this year, the effects were pronounced: an all but unpredicted recession and endless scandal, amounting to a political tax on the citizenry. "Soft" and sometimes tainted political contributions reached sums that in the aggregate represented a drag on the economy and a cost to the citizen consumer.

Japan needs more choice, though it is doubtful that Japan's establishment, with honorable exceptions, understands just how important that is to the future. Despite lip service to the notion of a responsible opposition capable of alternation in power, Japan's establishment treats political reform as postponable. In that belief they are like American politicos who wait for a *deus ex machina* to curb the deficit. Only in local politics, where there is often choice and alternation in power, is there much sense of responsiveness—severely constrained, however, by over-centralization of power in the central government bureaucracy in Tokyo.

That over-centralization is illustrated by the "seven-three" ratio in which the central bureaucracy controls 70 percent of local government expenditures and the local governments control 30 percent.

Japanese know all that but are hamstrung from doing much about it by the lack of political choice at the national level. The remarks of Japanese about politics are scathing, but until the explosion of popular anger in the fall of 1992, the most prominent reaction was apathy, exemplified by the July 1992 Upper House elections. Disgusted with cascading scandal and no longer certain of the relevance of electoral politics to their lives, many citizens stayed home; at 51 percent the voting rate for those elections was the lowest in postwar history.

The Consequences

The health of Japan's democratic institutions is not an academic issue. An electoral system that fosters massive soft campaign funds is as corrupting in Japan as it is in the United States. We would not say, for example, that the hold of the S&L lobby on the legislature and executive was without practical effect on Americans, who will pay for the S&L bailout for a generation. So too with Japan, where there are consequences for future domestic health and for Japan's uncertain engagement with the outside world, among them the near policy gridlock that blocks or delays decisions on all manner of issues whenever substantial change is involved. A justly praised Japanese desire for consensus, in the main a postwar phenomenon engendered by democratic reform, has degenerated into least-common-denominator politics.

In particular, this paper disputes conventional economic analysis that ascribes the lowering of Japan's discount rate in the mid to late 1980s to purely economic factors, mainly to offset the sharp rise in the value of the yen after the Plaza Accord of 1985 by providing low-cost capital to restructure significant sectors of Japanese industry. In fact, the 1980s' "bubble economy" that caused the current recession was in size and duration an essentially political phenomenon, the product of addiction to cheap money from which political contributions could be more readily secured. The conventional view is plausible at first glance; a temporary lowering of the discount rate was important to cushion the economy from the shock of the sharp rise in the yen. But to make record interest rate cuts in an economy then growing strongly at a minimum of 4 percent per annum and to keep them so low long beyond any economic justification were political decisions, designed to keep leading industrial sectors happy with cheap money and to keep soft campaign funds flowing, including new monies from the newly rich—among them prominent gangsters awash in funds from land speculation.

The "bubble"—an overheated economy, which at one time reached an 8 percent growth rate, coupled with an exponential increase in land and stock prices—was at its core political. That is why it was impossible for Japan to deflate the bubble before it reached dangerous proportions. The bubble was allowed to grow until 1989, when a major scandal (the Recruit affair) established a more sober climate, in which the Bank of Japan tightened credit and began the process of curbing speculative excess. The consequent recession has been deeper and of greater duration than it would have been had a more sensible approach to economic decision making been in vogue in Japan during the mid 1980s.

Japan's institutional performance has international consequences, making it harder to mesh its economy with that of the rest of the world and to decide its proper role in the post–Cold War era. Japan's insularity is rooted in culture and history, and the decline of its political institutions makes it even harder for it to deal with international issues. The usual examples—Japan's decisions about the Persian Gulf war and United Nations peacekeeping activities—may not be good ones; they touched upon the nature of the Japanese state and required time for debate. Better examples lie in delayed or blocked decisions on major economic matters, market openings, and improving the regulation of financial markets, where scandals have contributed to a loss of confidence in Japan's markets. Japan's inability to conduct a sustained effort to buy more from the rest of the world and bring Japan's trade surplus down to manageable proportions is linked to political stagnation.

In an example with some parallels to the United States, the response to Japan's recession was slow, the result of a politics of indecision despite the clear parliamentary majority the Liberal Democrats enjoy in budgetary matters. Even though there was a general understanding in business and financial circles that monetary policy alone would not do the trick and that a stimulus, budgetary and/or fiscal, to domestic demand was in order, the stately rhythms of decision making made it impossible to specify the amount and manner of the stimulus until late summer. Concerned about a falling stock market, Prime Minister Kiichi Miyazawa held a domestic "summit" on the economy just before the July

1992 Upper House election, but the summit confined itself to a restatement of the known—an unspecified stimulus come autumn.

Neither the promise nor a simultaneous cut in the discount rate stabilized the markets, which plunged again, though the announcement may have helped the LDP in the election. The new plunge energized the government to advance decisions to late summer 1992 on a major budgetary stimulus. The $86 billion dollar package aimed, among other things, at shoring up shaky bank assets through measures in some ways analogous to the S&L bailout in the United States. At this writing the markets have made something of a recovery; whether they will continue to recover is a subject of controversy. The view here is that the fundamentals of the Japanese economy will probably rebound by late 1993, but it will be hard for financial markets to regain stability unless they become less political and more transparent.

The sluggish decision making process—the product of bureaucratic infighting and political indecision—produced major international consequences, most prominent among them a sharply rising trade surplus, just at a time when Japan's buying power was needed to spur a lagging global economy. In a time of domestic recession, there is more focus on exports, as there has been in the United States; but the size of the Japanese trade surplus with the world, projected at $140 billion for 1992, is staggering. The new bubble, in exports, is unsustainable. Japan cannot go on selling so much abroad without buying more from overseas. As with the 1980s' "bubble" economy, the lancing of the export bubble is likely to be painful. Despite lower energy costs, key export industries will find it more difficult to sell goods abroad as the yen goes higher against the dollar and other currencies.

Where Will It Go?

The political situation may seem static to the casual observer, particularly after the recent Upper House election, which was distinguished by voter apathy and rather minor changes in the political map. But currents of change stir beneath the surface. The Japanese people have begun to react, however unsurely, to the unfairness engendered by persistent corruption. Though not certain, significant reform is possible—and likely by the end of the decade simply because society is evolving in so many other ways.

Today, the polls amply reflect that anger but show that the public remains somewhat confused about causes of political decline and focused on effects, such as the behavior of politicians and loose regulation of campaign finances, more than on systemic ills such as the manner of electing the Diet. There are unknowables, among them the capacity for reformers, who are found in both the ruling party and the opposition, to seize the moment for change. In the end, the prospects for major, early reform may rest on whether Japan's many-headed establishment has finally realized that reform is necessary to restore responsive government and public confidence.

Roughly speaking, there are four scenarios with respect to reform:

- A best-case scenario, **major reform soon**, would make politics more responsive and less corrupt. It could be described under three headings: electoral system change, decentralization of Japan's overly bureaucratized government, and political party realignment. In a way, Japanese have been like Americans were in the 1980s: faced with big problems but not generally cognizant of them. The body politic is, however, susceptible to shock. Some event, a scandal that becomes the "last straw," could fire the public and drive reform forward quickly. The Sagawa Kyubin affair, coupled with the effects of recession, may be that catalyst.

- A worst-case scenario, **apathy-atrophy**, represents the further decline of democratic institutions in favor of a Japanified corporate state, a modern-day *bakufu* (the governmental apparatus of the Shogunates, literally "camp administration") of accentuated feudal characteristics, preoccupied with political and bureaucratic ritual and insular and unresponsive to either its citizenry or international realities. In the past, scandals have run their course, bringing down major political figures but without forcing an examination of the underlying causes of political decay.

- A different worst-case scenario, the sum of all fears in Asia, sees the intimidating power of the far Right on the rise, pushing the clock back to an aggressive **remilitarized Japan**. The fears are understandable, and they have been heightened by the recent call of a Japanese military officer for a military coup to end corruption. That remains the least probable of all scenarios, however, because it would require, inter alia, a radical change in the peaceful temper of the Japanese.

- A fourth scenario begins with political stagnation in the short run, accompanied by gradual changes that drive major reform forward later in the decade as sub-surface currents in society grow in force and leadership passes to a new generation. Such a less than clear-cut outcome would have international consequences, an ambiguous Japanese posture with respect to post–Cold War policy, and the prospect of an even more uncomfortable role than the present one for America in pressing for changes in the economic arena.

When this was first written, the engines of reform had come together at a three-way stop sign, at which none could move before the others. Each one—electoral reform, decentralization, and political realignment—seemed contingent upon another's happening first. Neither recession nor scandal had been sufficient to overcome inertia. Perhaps the scandals were so frequent as to be numbing or, as with Americans and the S&Ls, too large to grasp.

Insiders have dismissed the effects of scandal as affecting individual politicians but not the course of politics. This time, they may be wrong. When this paper was first written, the most probable course appeared to be incremental reform; but in a September 1992 visit I was struck to hear Japanese, in casual conversation, complain about the apathy of their fellow citizens. Their complaints suggested that anger at the Sagawa affair was far more widespread than individual Japanese themselves had realized. Now that anger has exploded. The reaction to Sagawa, which ripped the veil off the influence of the *yakuza* (organized crime) in high politics, may become the shock that accelerates reform.

International Implications

For years, foreigners have worried about the health of American democracy because history has given them ample reason to believe that American politics affects them, for better or for worse. The interesting thing is that what happens to Japan's democracy is now also important to others. It is not just economic power that makes that so. For instance, it is generally understood in Asia—even in countries like China that are in no sense democratic—that democratic institutions and the "Peace Constitution" are a guarantee against feared resurgent Japanese militarism. In the far Pacific, the Japanese "model" has considerable attraction, though Japanese themselves are often distrusted. If the model runs into trouble, it has implications for neighbors.

On the great stage of the world, Japan's post–Cold War role in everything from the environment to U.N. peacekeeping is by no means defined, despite often sincere talk of internationalization. Political gridlock has made it more difficult to respond to the challenge of a swiftly changing world, which includes a relationship with the United States that appears to be in flux, a state in which neither country appears particularly happy, notwithstanding the significant benefits those ties confer on both nations.

In a brief examination of American diplomacy, this paper calls for establishing negotiating priorities, too often conspicuous by their absence; real support for a major role for Japan in global institutions, including a permanent seat in the U.N. Security Council; and a new framework for alliance—persuasive to publics in both countries. It also pleads for a sharp focus on the institutionalization of a Pacific community. The fortunes of the American people depend upon a peaceful and "open" Pacific, hospitable to trade and investment. There will be no "Pacific Century" without close, productive ties between Japan and the United States, and no such relationship is possible without a wider framework of Pacific and global cooperation.

Tensions in the U.S.-Japan relationship are visible, the result of psychological dislocation as well as differences in the way the two economies operate. There will always be friction, simply because of the sweep of interchange. But relations are likely to be especially troublesome in a climate of political stagnation because Tokyo elites will cling to the habit of recurring to foreign "pressure" (*gaiatsu*) as a catalyst for change that they themselves favor but are reluctant to endorse. Circumstances make it impossible for the United States to adopt a passive role, nor would most Japanese want that, whatever they think about American policies. For better or for worse, the United States will retain considerable influence, but from now on its effectiveness will depend heavily on persuasion, especially of the Japanese public.

Relations will be less troubled and our ideas more credible if we are "Changing Our Ways" (the title of the Carnegie Endowment's controversial proposals for American foreign policy) to reinvigorate American democracy and competitiveness. Many Japanese want to move beyond the Cold War and for a variety of reasons still look to America for leadership in crafting a modern vision for U.S.-Japan relations. The inauguration of the Clinton administration will provide a moment for statesmanship.

Seizing that opportunity will not end contention. But a new framework for alliance would change the psychology, lessen irritability, ease the task of negotiators, and make it easier for Japan to increase constructive engagement with the world at large.

The Scope of Inquiry

This paper begins with an outline of Japan's political development from the Meiji period, follows the rise of political parties and their submergence in a militarist tide, and describes the reforms of the American occupation and the evolution that followed after Japan regained its sovereignty. After assessing the achievements of postwar institutions, the study turns to the causes and consequences of political stagnation. The causes examined include the unwieldy mechanics of the Lower House electoral system, the ineffectiveness of the opposition, the over-concentration of power in Tokyo's central bureaucracy, and the "money politics" that has led to too-frequent corruption.

The consequences described in this paper center on the lack of a political choice (except at the local level where politics is often more responsive to the citizenry) that has led to growing voter apathy and disgust. There is a sense, all the more disturbing because it is new, that the system has become unfair to ordinary Japanese, whose standard of living has not grown in recent years. And there is the gridlock that often hamstrings Japan's decision making. Except for the lack of national political choice, those matters have a familiar ring for Americans. The paper concludes with an examination of scenarios for change and their prospects, followed by a few observations about the implications for Japan's international posture and for American policy and diplomacy.

Japan's Democracy—A Short Resume

The democratic ideal has demonstrated powerful appeal across many cultures—including those of Asia, as events have most recently shown in Thailand. The universal appeal of the principles of democracy has been accentuated by the ruin of competing ideologies and by an exponential increase in information flows among societies. The tradition of "top down" governance, derived in part from the millennial influence of Confucianism, continues to shape political institutions in Asia but has not suffocated the democratic impulse, even in China itself.

In the post–Cold War world, it is not out of place to suggest multicultural inquiry into the troubles of democracy, into ways to fix what's broken so that democratic government may grow more responsive to its citizens and to the challenges of a new era. Such inquiry has been largely confined to democratic transitions in developing countries, particularly in Latin America, and to the recent wave of democratization in the old Soviet empire. There is urgent need for dialogue about democracy among Asian and Western practitioners and observers, from which all cannot help but learn.

Some authors have indicated that Japan's feudal society under the Tokugawa Shogunate (1600–1863) shows what might be called pre-democratic traits, precursors of change. Sir George Sansom's monumental *History of Japan* says nothing about such traits, but demonstrates that the rise of the merchants and the de facto breakdown of class distinctions between merchants and samurai (the warrior class, the top rung in Japan's feudal system) in the latter stages of the Tokugawas paved the way for the modernization of Japan in the Meiji era.

In his early, often critical study of the American occupation, *Japan's American Interlude,* Kazuo Kawai went further, to argue that political Confucianism took a different form in Japan than in China, postulating reciprocal obligations between the ruled and their rulers, in contrast to what he saw as a one-way street of filial obligations to the rulers of China. Others would argue that Kawai overstated the difference, but whatever the case, in Kawai's view, the notion of reciprocal obligations between the ruled and their rulers was a "democratic" feature that made Japan more receptive to the political changes that were to come.

More recently, Junichi Kyogoku in *The Political Dynamics of Japan* pointed out that the idea of the common good is inherent in the strong sense of group identity among Tokugawa-era communities. Foreign observers, it should be said, see that group sense as posing a danger of a recurrence of exaggerated nationalism. Perhaps, but as Kyogoku went on to say, intense loyalty to the small group, the business enterprise, the political faction, the bureaucracy of a particular ministry of government can also clash with devotion to country. To put it in different words, "we the village" and "we the people" may conflict, as seen in the behavior of the Ministry of Finance in recent scandals in the financial markets.

Historians such as Edwin O. Reischauer and W. G. Beasley have remarked on the paradox of an insular Japan that nonetheless encounters turning points precisely in moments of engagement with the outside world. Certainly, geography has been destiny. The insularity that has made it difficult for Japan to engage the outside world in the post–Cold War era has its origins in the relative isolation, until the modern era, of the main islands of Japan from all but sporadic foreign influences. The first to be recorded came between the sixth and ninth centuries with the introduction from Korea and China of Buddhism, Confucianism, and a writing system. In the late thirteenth century, Japan fought off successive Mongol invasions with the help of a fortuitous typhoon, the *kamikaze*, or "divine wind," that helped foster Japan's sense of exceptionalism; but an exhausted state then fell prey to a century of civil war.

In the late sixteenth century Spanish and Portuguese traders and missionaries were at first welcomed, but in the early seventeenth century the new Tokugawa Shoguns imposed self-seclusion (*sakkoku*). Fearful the flag and the sword would follow trade and the cross, as they had in the Philippines and on the coast of China, the Tokugawas violently suppressed Christianity and closed down Western contact except for the small Dutch trading post at Deshima in southern Japan. Even so, *rangaku* (Dutch learning) stimulated venturesome minds in medicine, science, and economic and military matters. Japan's willingness to experiment with democracy owes something to a tradition of at least two millennia in which Japan and individual Japanese, despite an insular society, took an eclectic posture towards foreign ideas, accepting some, rejecting others, and making yet others their own—but only after transforming them.

The Sources of Modernity: The Meiji Period (1867–1912)

Modern Japan begins with Meiji, a period of revolutionary, but by no means democratic, change. The history of Japan's fitful experiment with institutions of democracy (elections, a parliament, and cabinet government) begins at that time. The Meiji Restoration, so called because its ideology demanded "restoration" of the young emperor to the pinnacle of Japan's polity, a place his ancestors had not come near to occupying for nearly a millennium, was sparked by two events, one native and one foreign: the decay of Tokugawa rule and a coincident challenge from the West to a Japan secluded for two centuries from Western contact.

The discontented *samurai* from outlying fiefdoms who forced out the Tokugawas agreed with the Tokugawa diagnosis of a threat from the West, but had come to recognize by the time they took power that self-seclusion was impossible; Japan was too weak to enforce it. Under the slogan of "strength and wealth," the Meiji leadership undertook to modernize Japan as quickly as possible in order to ensure that Japan would not fall prey, as China had, to Western colonialism. Remarkably successful in many respects, the new oligarchy swiftly abolished the feudal system, including serfdom and the *samurai* class itself, drove forward rapid industrialization, and spurred economic growth. They also built a conscript military and, by the beginning of the twentieth century, had emulated one of the West's less-attractive practices—colonial expansion—in Korea and Manchuria, in time defeating Korean, Chinese, and Russian forces.

In the first decades of Meiji, American influence was small, notwithstanding the importance of Commodore Matthew C. Perry and the diplomat Townsend Harris in opening trade with the West. While America was occupied with its Civil War and Reconstruction, the major influences on Japan were German, French, British, and Russian (with Russia a growing enemy). The Meiji rulers were eclectic: The British built the first railroads and trained the navy, and the French first trained the army. The new system's political institutions, except for their mythic Shinto underpinning, were largely derived from the practices of Prussia, which the Meiji rulers had studied personally and had found congenial to their drive to modernize from the top down.

The authoritarian Meiji constitution of 1889 was largely devised by German advisors—just as, in dissimilar circumstances, the American occupation authorities inspired a goodly part of the current Japanese constitution. Bureaucracy antedated Meiji, going back to the Confucian-inspired imperial courts of the first millennium, as did respect for education—the first schools to prepare *samurai* for administration date to the seventeenth century. But the new rulers did not look to replace the *bakufu*—the Tokugawa bureaucracy, hereditarily restricted to *samurai*—with the Chinese tradition of entry into government through examinations on the Confucian classics. Intent on modernization, the Meiji rulers modeled the style of exams and the structure of the bureaucracy on German practices, setting up the exam-based institutions from which today's bureaucracy is directly descended.

The Meiji ideology, however, was singularly Japanese, its mythic rationale derived from Tokugawa-era neo-Confucian scholars opposed to "official" Buddhism and the politically correct Confucianism that prescribed filial loyalty to the Tokugawas. Over time, neo-Confucians had fused the native tradition of Shinto and the Confucian ethic into an exceptionalist doctrine, often called the *Nihonjinron*. Nativist scholars claimed that Confucian philosophy had a "Japaneseness" to it; some even said Confucius must have been Japanese and the true "Central Kingdom" was Japan, not China. They revered the emperor and looked upon the Tokugawas as usurpers. Those ideas evolved into what became the mythical rationale for the new regime, which exalted Shinto as a state religion and the emperor as its expression, though the oligarchy was careful to circumscribe the power of the Meiji emperor himself and his successors.

The early Meiji approach had about it little that was democratic, except for an egalitarian emphasis on universal education and the exam-based meritocracy that by the end of the century was opening up Japan's establishment. There were other intellectual currents, inspired by contact with the West and by the change sweeping across Japan, that took a more liberal approach. It is noteworthy, for example, that John Stuart Mill was perhaps the most admired of foreign authors during the Meiji period. There was discontent with the grasp of a self-selected oligarchy upon Japan. In a few provinces, disaffected ex-*samurai* and merchants formed the first political parties in the early 1870s, in some sense a continuation of the controlled tension between Tokyo and local interests that flared from time to time in feudal days and that has again become a political issue in the 1990s.

The Meiji constitution was promulgated as an act of imperial grace and was inspired by a desire to regularize the forms of government in a way that would make the West treat Japan as a normal state. But in providing for parties, an elected parliament (called the Diet in translation, in testimony to the Germanic influence), and cabinets (at first dissociated from the legislative parties), the leadership was also yielding to elite pressures for wider participation in government. Despite many less-than-democratic features in the constitution, there was a de facto devolution of day-to-day power toward the parties, which accrued influence through ties with business, a practice restored in postwar Japan. The budget gave Meiji legislators the lever; in the absence of parliamentary approval for a new budget, the previous year's budget remained in effect (a kind of "continuing resolution"). In a time when growth demanded an expansionary budget, the Meiji oligarchs saw necessity, if not virtue, in bringing the parties into the cabinet. Later, parties began to lead the cabinet.

By the end of the nineteenth century, British and American political influence had assumed more importance. American influence became especially great after the Russo-Japanese War, when Theodore Roosevelt mediated the Portsmouth Treaty of peace in 1905, which confirmed Japan's colonial interests in Manchuria. There was an evident correlation between Japan's growing ties with Great Britain and the United States in the latter part of the Meiji era and the devolution of power toward the parliament and cabinet. Following Japan's alliance with Britain, France, and the United States in World War I, the political system had evolved by the mid-1920s to the point at which parties were strong and the custom of party-led cabinets seemingly entrenched. In 1925, universal manhood suffrage replaced the earlier property-based electorate. (It took the American occupation to extend suffrage to women.)

The emperor, rather than the people, remained the fount of legitimacy, notwithstanding his lack of power. In practice, two governments, one civil and one military, reported separately to him, a constraint that was to prove fatal to elected government. By the 1930s, the rise of the military, the subordination of the nation to colonial ambition in China, and growing strain with the United States had put intolerable pressure on Japan's parliamentary experiment. The strains were intensified by restrictive U.S. immigration legislation, which sparked resentment in Japan at the racism that imbued those laws. The Japanese military chafed at the Washington Naval Treaty of 1922, which established a 10:10:6 ratio for capital ships among the United States, Britain, and Japan—a restriction that the Japanese would later ignore. But it was

America's strong opposition to Japan's colonial expansion that set the two countries on a collision course.

There were other causes for the death of democratic practices, among them a worldwide depression and the corruption that became a rallying cry against politicians and the business establishment. The coup de grace was delivered by a violent nationalism among younger army officers, often from rural provinces, imperfectly educated and resentful of Tokyo elites and "corrupt" Western influence. The parties and even the military leadership were cowed by periodic assassinations as the hotheads among the military drove the country to greater military adventures in China, even though the radicals never held the top military posts. Japan became a formal ally of Nazi Germany, and as the vise of war closed, the government abolished the parties and created the Imperial Rule Assistance Association, a Japanese variant of the single political front common to fascist and communist regimes. The parties for the most part acquiesced without protest.

To the extent that postwar democracy has worked in Japan, it is due not only to occupation reforms and the subsequent evolution of those institutions, but to the legacy of earlier, failed experimentation with a parliamentary system that began in the Meiji era and continued into the 1930s. The imperfect institutions of prewar times gave the Japanese experience with democratic practices, including a sense of what had gone wrong, to draw upon in the postwar period. Not a few of the postwar political class got their training in party politics in the late 1920s and early 1930s, before the military closed down the parties for all practical purposes. With one exception, the major parties trace their complicated ancestry to one or more of the prewar parties.

The American Occupation: 1945–1952

Japan's spectacular postwar rise to prosperity could not have happened without the end of militarism, the police state, and the cult of the emperor. But the occupation did more than simply overthrow the institutions that had led Japan to war. General Douglas MacArthur and his advisors set out to replace them with a democratic system of government. Some of the occupation's decisions were wrong-headed; others remain controversial. But in the main the occupation was successful, a tribute to the wisdom and tolerance of conquerors and conquered. The lessons of Versailles had been learned. Not only in Europe, where the task was marginally easier, but in the Far East enemies were turned into friends and despotism replaced by democratic institutions.

In Japan, democratic institutions and reforms gave everyone a stake in the future, built up the middle class, fostered rural prosperity, and provided a climate in which reconstruction and growth could flourish. MacArthur's refusal to allow the Soviets to play a role in the occupation meant that, unlike Germany, there was no undigestible division of the nation to cast a long shadow upon political development.

The importance of the occupation's land reform cannot be overstated. Land reform increased agricultural productivity and turned peasants into small landowners with a stake in the future. Without that most democratic of reforms, Japan's economic miracle would not have occurred. (Ironically, the reform's author, Wolf Ladejinsky, became a target of McCarthyism even though the Japanese farmers themselves became staunch conservative voters, providing the LDP with an unshakable electoral base until recent years.) It is important to emphasize the economic importance of democracy, because a strain in Japanese conservatism doggedly rewrites history, glossing over Japan's colonial behavior in Asia, to resurrect a modern version of the *Nihonjinron*. To oversimplify, that version has two elements: that Japan could not have done anything truly bad (hence the effort to deny the past) and its exceptionalist corollary, that good things are always native born.[2]

According to the ultra-conservative rewrite, occupation reforms had nothing to do with Japan's economic "miracle"; rather, it was the wartime control economy that laid the basis for Japan's postwar growth. In the war of words over Japan, combatants such as Dutch journalist Karel van Wolferen, in *The Enigma of Japanese Power*, eloquently take apart the *Nihonjinron*, but rather uncritically accept its version of events, in which the control economy provided the blueprint for economic success.[3]

It is breathtaking to suggest that wartime policies were responsible for postwar growth. The war economy was Japan's Achilles' heel, as unsuitable for sustained conflict as for peace. It resembled the late command economy of the Soviets, dedicated to military production and to colonial autarky, trading with conquered possessions just as the Soviets conducted command trade with Eastern Europe.

To be sure, Japan's economic miracle was not an American gift, though the occupation gave it an important boost. Economic growth had its origins in Meiji. The work ethic went back further, to Confucius and his reinterpreters, both Chinese and Japanese. There is a striking comparison between the stimulus the Protestant ethic gave to European capitalism, as described in R. L. H. Tawney's *Religion and the Rise of Capitalism* and Max Weber's *The Protestant Ethic and Capitalism*, and that which Confucianism gave to the modern work ethic in Asia, from Singapore in the south to Japan and Korea in the north. Confucianism long antedated the Industrial Revolution; it is obvious that other influences were at play, especially the rise of the merchant class in Tokugawa Japan and the challenge of modernization imposed by engagement with the West.

It was in Meiji that cooperation among business, bureaucracy, and government got its start. So did industrial policy, particularly the emphasis on infrastructure, the heart of the developmental model that Japanese today urge on poor nations. The *zaibatsu* (industrial conglomerations) took shape in Meiji. Their heirs, transformed, are the *keiretsu*, today a word with greater currency among foreign observers than among Japanese, who call them *grupu*, from the English "group." Like the Meiji rulers, the occupation, concerned that Japan's war-ravaged economy not drain the U.S treasury, mandated protectionism to shelter industries. The "infants" did not shed protectionism until they grew into gorillas in the marketplace, but that is another story.

The postwar "capitalist developmental state," described in Chalmers Johnson's seminal work *MITI and the Japanese Miracle*, relied on intimate cooperation between industry and bureaucrats, many involved in the wartime "control economy." But industrial policy focused not on autarky but on export-led growth, an idea foreign to *comprador* policies of the military state. Quality was a postwar industrial policy to redress Japan's prewar reputation for shoddy goods, as officials at the Japan Productivity Center explained to me in 1958. The technology of quality, imported from the U.S., owed much to centuries of Japanese emphasis on harmonious group efforts.

In sum, Japan's postwar success is due to an amalgam of historical influences. Native cultural traits mingled with Western influence, most prominently in the Meiji era and in the postwar reforms, which proved congenial to the temper of the Japanese people. Economic assistance to a prostrate Japan was important in keeping the Japanese alive; the fiscal austerity imposed by the occupation (the "Dodge mission") laid a basis for recovery; and the importation of technology helped industrial development.

The most important contribution of General MacArthur's occupation lay in sweeping democratic reforms, which established sovereignty in the people and all manner of political rights, without which the road to prosperity would have been more difficult, if not impossible. Article IX of the constitution, renouncing war as an instrument of policy, is for many Japanese the emotional equivalent of the U.S. First Amendment, but would have been meaningless without the guarantees of political and personal liberties conferred by a constitution that remains intact long after MacArthur and his occupation faded away. Those liberties have proved congenial to the Japanese people—and that is why so many are frustrated by the current state of their politics.

The "Reverse Course" (1952–1960)

A lingering addiction to the authoritarian political organization of the military era became contentious immediately after the occupation. Civilian politicians and bureaucrats, particularly those whose political rights had been restored after having been "purged" from public life by the occupation, sought to institute a "reverse course," as Japanese critics styled it, "to correct the excesses of democratization of postwar reforms." They forced out Shigeru Yoshida, the occupation-era prime minister, took the reins of government, and sought legislative changes to restore, as they saw it, an orderly, harmonious—and controlled—society.

The "reverse course" was a hot topic when I first worked in Japan in the late 1950s. Japanese contemporaries worried that the newly minted LDP (formed in 1955 through the fusion of two conservative parties) would push the clock back to authoritarianism. It is one of the ironies of postwar history that the Japan Socialist Party, formed at the same time through a fusion of leftist parties, was always a staunch defender of occupation reforms even as it moved further and further to the Left in opposition to Japan's alliance with the United States.

The "reverse course" took hold in education, recentralized under an archaic Ministry of Education. Through the exercise of democratic rights, freedom of the press, freedom of assembly, and parliamentary contention, however, the people blocked much of the "reverse course" thrust. For example, for practical as well as philosophical reasons the government reversed the occupation edict that decentralized the police; but when Prime Minister Nobusuke Kishi sought to strengthen police powers in 1957, the legislation summoned up unwanted memories of prewar police abuses and the consent of the governed was unobtainable. In the face of massive demonstrations, universal condemnation from press and opposition parties, and dissension in Kishi's own party, the government eventually withdrew the bill.

In the 1960s, however, in the words of Professor Kyogoku, the LDP gave up "reviving the prewar political system" to become "a conservative party that accepts the influx and spread of mass culture and Westernized modes of social life." That change came about in response to contention over policy within the establishment and society in general. The climax came in 1960 at the time of the then controversial revision of the Security Treaty when demonstrations forced the cancellation of President Dwight Eisenhower's visit. Weakened by controversy over foreign as well as domestic policy, Kishi resigned.

Hayato Ikeda, Kishi's chief critic within the party, became prime minister with a mandate for a quite different, economically focused agenda, which commanded ample public support and bolstered the LDP's electoral fortunes. Ikeda's "income doubling" plan worked far better than even its architects had imagined, as one of them, Saburo Okita, observed to me. Politically, Ikeda and his followers, one-time associates of Yoshida, were more accepting of the diversity spawned by democratic reforms. Years later, Masayoshi Ohira, an Ikeda lieutenant and later prime minister, commented to me about the complaints of hardline conservatives about a supposed lack of discipline in society: "That is only attainable in war—do they want that again?"

One hears echoes of the "reverse course," though the phrase has fallen into disuse, in the trial balloon of a few conservatives for a "grand coalition" of conservatives and socialists to break the parliamentary deadlock in the Upper House. The notion, roundly criticized when it appeared, has a superficial origin in the postwar West German model, which started the rise to power of the Social Democrats under Willy Brandt. The psychology, however, seems akin to that of Japan's old Imperial Rule Assistance Association, seeking harmonious ratification of government policy.

Weighing the Achievements

Much Western criticism of Japan, accurate as it often is in particulars, is ethnocentric, comparing Japanese practice not to the imperfect conduct of Euro-American democracies, but to ideal norms. In democracy's untidy house, there are many mansions, parliamentary systems, presidential and federal systems, proportional representation, single-member districts, and so on. Working constitutional protections for civil liberties are a sine qua non, but some liberties are protected better than others, depending on the country. We need to look at Japan through the same lens, focused on the performance of democratic institutions, through which we view ourselves and Western Europe. The minimum standard encompasses the following:

- Free, honest, and periodic elections to choose (and change, if we wish) governments, through a secret ballot in conditions of universal suffrage, the ballot accompanied by rights essential to the proper conduct of elections—for example, political parties, liberty of campaigning, and effective freedom of speech.

- Fundamental protection for the rights of individuals, particularly from their rulers, and the general observance of those rights.

In those terms, Japan did reasonably well for much of the postwar period; many of the problems discussed in these pages have become acute only in recent years. To begin with, elections are honestly counted ("vote early and often" is not a Japanese phenomenon). Outright buying of votes has all but disappeared; candidates—from government and opposition alike—are everywhere. Parties campaign freely, and freedom of speech and assembly is protected.

With respect to individual rights, the contrast between postwar and wartime Japan, with its thought police (*tokko*) and political detentions, could not be greater. Today experiments are not performed upon prisoners, nor are women rounded up to "comfort" the soldiery. The great evils of militarism are gone—too much forgotten in the historical amnesia fostered by the Ministry of Education, but gone nonetheless. Freedom of speech exists for the politically incorrect as well as for the conforming public. More police abuses exist than most Japanese admit—particularly intimidation of suspects—but they are less spectacular than those in, say, Los Angeles. In fact, police restraint has generally marked the postwar period. In the huge political riots of the fifties and sixties, only one student died—none were gunned down, as were students at Kent State.

Despite unhealthy self-censorship, the news media have been vigorous critics. (Western criticism of the herd instinct in Japan's media is on target, but could be as easily applied to our own press.) Press exposure of major scandals brings down governments. In a case reminiscent of Watergate, media exposure forced out Prime Minister Kakuei Tanaka in 1974. Later Tanaka was convicted of taking bribes from the Lockheed Corporation; the press made it impossible to look the other way. In 1989, exposure of the Recruit scandal forced Prime Minister Noboru Takeshita to resign, not so much for personal involvement but to take responsibility for the climate of impropriety that characterized the Recruit affair. His successor, Sosuke Uno, was driven out in two months because of his widely publicized unchivalrous behavior towards a former mistress.

Social discrimination against outsiders, most notably the large minority of long-time Korean residents, remains an unpleasant fact. Ancient prejudices remain against descendants of Japan's version of "untouchables," who performed services, like the tanning of hides, that were taboo in Japanese lore. Racial prejudice is a reality too often reflected in the public remarks of public men. With respect to foreigners in general, despite the closed social patterns, the story is complex and changing. For every story a foreigner tells of rejection, there are a dozen stories of kindness, of Japanese who go out of their way to be helpful to strangers in their land.

Japan's low rate of violent crime, the result of cultural mores and strict gun control, is the envy of the world. The power of organized crime (the *yakuza*), often linked to politicians—particularly but not exclusively in the ruling party—has grown disturbingly but is not as potent as that of the Mafia in Italy. The far Right, financed by shadowy businessmen, is intimidating, as evidenced by attempted assassinations of the mayor of Nagasaki and of LDP elder Shin Kanemaru, but it hardly has any electoral backing, far less than that of Jean-Marie Le Pen in France. The Japanese people, through the exercise of their liberties, time and again have rebuffed the essays of some conservatives to change the "Peace Constitution" to permit a more assertive military. The fears of Asians are understandable, but there is today no resurgent militarism in Japan.

For years democratic institutions worked well on behalf of a public consensus behind reconstruction, recovery, sustained growth, and the recuperation of national self-esteem. The goals were not static; they inspired enormous change that was led by politicians, implemented by a talented bureaucracy, and supported by the people. The alliance among business, bureaucracy, and ruling party rested on the consent of the governed—not only in honest elections, but also in high savings rates, a

Japanese disposition to work killing hours, and a high degree of labor peace in the private, productive sector.

For a time after 1955, there operated in Japan a much less malign version of the Southern White Primary in the Democratic Party in the southern United States (see V. O. Key's *Southern Politics in State and Nation*). Leadership and basic policy decisions were worked out within a single party, the ruling LDP, in which leadership and factional struggle involved policy change as well as personal ambition. No citizen was disenfranchised, in contrast to the Southern White Primary's exclusion of blacks, and the electoral system, notwithstanding its quirks, then provided accountable government. Prime ministers came to power with explicit policy agendas, and the clash of agendas played a role in their departure and in the selection of a successor.

In the manner of successful parties everywhere, as Gerald L. Curtis pointed out in *The Japanese Way of Politics*, the LDP demonstrated responsiveness to changing national needs and popular aspirations. It is all but forgotten now, but until the 1970s there was vigorous contention over Japan's foreign policy, based on alliance with America. In those days the polls consistently showed that a majority of the Japanese preferred something less than the LDP's policy of close alliance: either less U.S. military presence, as the small Democratic Socialist and Komeito parties advocated in different formulations, or the abstract neutrality of the major opposition, the Socialists. In election after election a majority supported the LDP for its domestic skills, though people were not entirely happy with foreign policy. In so doing, Japanese showed they were not so different from Americans as they claim; voters gave priority to domestic issues. In the LDP's capacity to adapt policy to a changing society lay the key to electoral success.

In the early 1970s, the end of the Vietnam War, the reversion of Okinawa to Japanese sovereignty, and the U.S. and Japanese rapprochement with China brought about a significant change in popular attitudes toward close alliance with the United States, which became more and more acceptable as it focused primarily on the Soviet Union and North Korea, countries that, unlike China and Vietnam, appeared to the Japanese public to be proper subjects for the policy of containment.

Majorities also came to believe that Japan's Self-Defense Forces were acceptable, did not spell a return to militarism, and were as a consequence compatible with the constitution, so long as they remained confined to a strictly defensive role, as they have been. In another evidence of pragmatism, the LDP leadership, whatever the views of individual leaders, chose not to confront the public's opposition to change in the "Peace Constitution," despite constant pressure from the Right of the party and the expedient remarks of a few Americans, often civilian strategists preoccupied with "burden sharing," that Japan ought to revise the prohibition in order to contribute more heavily to Cold War military concerns.

The Lack of Political Choice

Japan's political stagnation stems from the lack of practical choice at the national level. No opposition party or combination of them is today in shape to capitalize on discontent with one-party rule. While the opposition cannot escape censure for its role, the principal cause for the lack of choice is systemic, an increasingly dysfunctional electoral system that decreases competition between the ruling party and its opponents and that fosters soft campaign funds and corrosive scandal.

In the bicameral Diet, as in the British House of Commons, the Lower House predominates and is supposed to directly represent the populace. Unless the government chooses to dissolve the Lower House earlier, which is usually the case, general elections must be held every four years. The Lower House has untrammelled authority over budgets and treaties and chooses the prime minister. The Upper House (the House of Councillors) is subordinate but not toothless; it can block ordinary legislation unless the Lower House musters a two-thirds vote to override, and it serves as an institutional check on cabinet government, though that role is nowhere specified in the constitution. Every three years half the Upper House seats are up for election, through a mixture of regional contests and nationwide proportional representation.

In what dean of America's Asia scholars Robert Scalapino called Japan's "one and a half party system" there are several opposition parties. They win seats; for the first time, in the 1989 Upper House election several opposition parties, fueled by voter discontent over the Recruit scandal and a value added–style tax, in total won more seats than the LDP. That shift led to Japanese-style "divided government"—really semi-divided—in which the ruling party had to engineer ad hoc coalitions with two small opposition parties to pass ordinary legislation through the Upper House. Three years later, in balloting for the other half of the Upper House seats, which were at stake in the July 1992 election, the voters had a chance to force change. They chose the status quo. In a contest distinguished by apathy, the LDP lost six seats out of its seventy-five at stake, not enough to alter the existing balance and nothing like the beating the LDP had suffered three years earlier.

The Eternal Opposition

In the dominant Lower House the LDP has held continuous sway. Neither alone nor in combination have the opposition parties prepared themselves to take power. Instead, they have become addicted to privilege and the access to patronage conferred by the workings of an electoral system that almost guarantees the opposition a substantial share of seats. Except for the question of constitutional revision, by the mid 1970s the banners under which the principal opposition, the Japan Socialist Party (JSP),[4] had campaigned were no longer relevant. For the average Japanese, neither alliance with the United States nor the existence of self-defense forces were any longer at issue.

The JSP continued to campaign as if they were. Socialist policy was hostage to its major constituency, the radical public-sector unions in the Sohyo labor confederation, where the litmus test depended on Marxist attitudes whose time had passed. As a consequence, the JSP never found its Bad Godesberg (the German spa where in the 1950s Willy Brandt and his Social Democrats rid themselves of Marxist ideology to become a modern democratic party). In private, JSP parliamentarians became more realistic about domestic and international policy (and cynical towards their party), but the party platform remained congealed in the amber of 1920s Marxism.

While changes in popular attitudes spelled the end of Socialist challenge, contention did not end. The LDP once found it necessary to go into coalition with a minor party to achieve a parliamentary majority in the dominant Lower House. But except on one crucial issue, that of constitutional revision, the major opposition party, the Socialists, ceased to represent major policy stances important to the people. The small parties were more focused on domestic issues, but ideological and policy differences made coalition impossible, except on a case-by-case basis, usually in opposition to some proposed government legislation.

In response to the end of the Cold War and the scandal-caused decline in LDP prestige, the Socialists sought to end their own decline. They selected a woman, the dynamic Takako Doi, to chair the party. Her stewardship began well with the victory in the 1989 Upper House elections, but ended in failure because the JSP could not develop a modern, coherent program. In Lower House elections the next year the JSP did badly, taking up the banner of protectionism in front of an electorate mostly made up of consumers, who are increasingly aware that they are shortchanged in Japan's economic miracle.

After a loss in the Tokyo gubernatorial election, Ms. Doi resigned. She left a long-term legacy: the arrival to elective office—particularly local—of numbers of articulate, intelligent women from the Socialist Party. Today a breath of fresh air, tomorrow they could help renovate politics. The optimism is tempered, however, by the fact that the new leadership, under Chairman Makoto Tanabe, returned to a men's club atmosphere. Only a handful of women were candidates in the July Upper House elections, a factor, though not the major one, in the JSP's poor showing. The new leadership fared badly, becoming the object of ridicule because of delaying tactics used to oppose any form of Japanese participation in U.N. peacekeeping. The JSP's vote in the July Upper House contest fell to 13 percent, the lowest ever. Though the party retained its twenty-two seats at stake, they were far fewer than the Socialists had won three years earlier. The party's future is in doubt.

The Small Parties

The Japan Communist Party (JCP), aided by a protest vote from non-members, has regularly won a small share of seats. A Eurocommunist stance never developed, however, despite the slogan of a "lovable communist party" (*aisareru kyosanto*). An "independent" foreign policy—critical of the U.S., the Soviet Union, and China—had theoretical attraction, but the JCP's rigid Leninist centralism appealed to no one but party faithful, and the collapse of communism has put the JCP on the skids.

Two small, moderate opposition parties, the Democratic Socialists (DSP) and the Komeito (Clean Government Party), never fulfilled the potential that some Japanese and Western observers saw in them. The DSP, formed in a Socialist split over the 1960 Security Treaty with the United States, enjoys private-sector labor backing and modest support from business, which saw the DSP as a check upon the ideological Socialists. The DSP often suggests constructive changes to government legislation, most recently in the long debate over how and whether Japan should participate in U.N. peacekeeping activities. But while European and American observers found in the "moderate" DSP a view congenial to politics as practiced in the West, Japanese voters saw the DSP as neither fish nor fowl. The party has been in recurring danger of extinction, kept alive by a frayed core constituency among private-sector labor unions.

In the late 1960s the Komeito was founded by the Sokka Gakkai, a large lay organization of the Nichiren sect of Buddhism. To many Japanese and Western observers, the Komeito seemed to be cresting a tide of "new religions" appealing to the alienated and uncertain. The reality was otherwise. In an increasingly satisfied Japan, "new religions" did not keep growing. Despite sensible efforts to broaden support among nonbelievers, particularly urban voters on the margins of prosperity, the Komeito reached a ceiling. Most Japanese did not find a sectarian party attractive. Scandal (particularly sub rosa contributions from the LDP leadership) stained the party's clean-government banner. A recent split between temple and party threatened the Komeito's sectarian base, but predictions of the party's demise are premature, though its flirtation with coalition with the LDP is not exactly a message of reform.

In 1969, young, articulate freshman LDP Diet members with ideas of their own ran up against the wall of seniority in a party showing the effects of scandal. The sense that a country without a real opposition was ripe for the formation of a moderate alternative to the LDP led them to form the New Liberal Club (*Shin Jiyu Kurabu*) in 1975. Led by one of Japan's more attractive politicians, Yohei Kono, the NLC sought to provoke the oft-predicted "great restructuring" of Japanese politics. In one close election, the NLC held the balance and were invited by the LDP to join the cabinet to provide a parliamentary majority. That prompted hopes that the NLC, if it could not become the magnet for a new majority, might play the role of the West German Free Democrats as an essential coalition partner in any government. In the next election, however, the LDP went after the New Liberals and wiped out most of their seats.

In 1986, those who were left rejoined the LDP, ending a decade's experiment. There are learned explanations for the NLC's failure. They range from the sociological (the presumed nature of the Japanese voter) to the personal (rivalries in a party too small to afford them). The explanation offered by a senior Japanese newsman and by a businessman is more direct: Business never contributed enough money to the New Liberals to permit nationwide campaigns. On the moderate left, a similar phenomenon occurred in 1977: the formation of the Shaminren (translated as the Social Democratic League, but better described as Social Populists.) Its message, social welfare capitalism, drew approval from intellectuals and commentators, but not from voters. The Shaminren won no seats in the July Upper House election.

For the last three years, the most interesting alternative was Rengo, the Japan Confederation of Trade Unions' endorsed candidates for the Upper House. In the 1989 elections Rengo selected good candidates, independents and popular figures from the labor movement, the latter from both the Socialists and the DSP, and secured the agreement of noncommunist opposition parties to refrain from running candidates in districts where Rengo had entered the lists. Rengo won in each of twelve contests.

Rengo's problem was the reverse of that faced by the NLC: Rengo had candidates but no common policy stance. Confronted with an issue that divided its parliamentarians, whether to oppose with the JSP the peacekeeping legislation or to support the version as amended by the DSP and the Komeito, Rengo temporized. Despite early predictions that it would do well in the July 1992 Upper House elections, Rengo won not a seat. In contrast, the two small parties that played a constructive role in the legislative outcome of the peacekeeping debate did a little better than expected; the Komeito picked up several seats and the DSP added a seat when it was expected to lose two or three.

The sad electoral history of new parties notwithstanding, another venture is underway, fueled by the attention of the media, hopeful as always that something will come along to rejuvenate politics. The New Japan Party is headed by former LDP governor Morihiro Hosokawa of Kumamoto. Hosokawa argues that the post-modern Japanese are ready for a new politics. His advocacy of governmental decentralization struck a responsive chord, and in the Upper House election four of his party's ten candidates won seats. That result was ballyhooed in the Japanese press (echoed by Western media), but it was in fact a relatively modest victory, nothing like Rengo's success three years earlier. The real test for the New Japan Party will come in the next Lower House election.

The widely cited off-the-record remark of a senior LDP figure that "Red is dead" was understood to mean that Japanese might now vote for an opposition government because there is no reason to be scared, now that ideology matters so little. Perhaps, but in the last Upper House elections, the voters gave no evidence to support that judgment. In July's contest, two electoral rules of thumb clashed: the lower the voting rate, the better for the opposition vs. economic trouble means more votes for the ruling LDP, thought to be the better economic managers. The economy won out.

The Lower House Electoral System

It would be hard to exaggerate the responsibility of the opposition for its plight, but the mathematics of an idiosyncratic electoral system for the Lower House provide the most important single cause of political stagnation. The Japanese call the system inherited from Meiji a "mid-sized electoral district system" (*chuosenkyoku seido*) to distinguish it from common alternatives—the single-member districts of the British House of Commons and the U.S. House of Representatives, and the proportional representation in use in much of continental Europe. The system shares with the single-member districts the distinction of producing working governments. With proportional representation it shares the assurance that an opposition will have significant representation, a de facto guarantee of the more than one-third of the Lower House necessary to block constitutional revision or an override of an Upper House vote against government-sponsored legislation.

Districts range from two to six members (three to five, usually). A less-than-democratic feature is the weight given to less-populous districts, usually rural, that helped the LDP maintain a Lower House majority in good times and bad. Periodically, the Diet legislates redistricting but has never caught up with demographics. Today, rural weighting has less effect on electoral outcomes because of changing demographics: a population that has shifted from largely rural to urban and semi-urban (Japan's rural population is only about 25 percent, compared with 75 percent in the late 1940s).

The demographic shift was counterbalanced by a modest shift in urban votes toward the LDP, which preserved the party's relative majority in the popular vote so that the LDP, even when the NLC took votes from it, never fell out of the 40 percent range. Still, a vote in the least-populous district (which happens to be in Tokyo) is worth four times as much as a vote in the most-populous district. The government is under court edict to conduct yet another modest redistricting before the next Lower House election.

The worst feature of the system, however, is that the citizen only votes for one candidate, so that a candidate usually needs no more than 12–15 percent of the vote to get elected. The system *diminishes* competition among parties. It promotes competition among conservatives instead, who fight each other for what in most districts is a fairly predictable percentage of conservative votes.

There is something akin to an econometric relationship between the number of conservative candidates in a district and the number of seats the conservatives win. When there are "too many" conservative candidates, "electoral chaos" (*ranritsu*) ensues and the LDP loses a seat it would otherwise win. The fragmented opposition knows it will get a share of the seats, which may increase or decrease depending on public mood and the attractiveness of candidates. Since winning a seat requires only a small percentage of the vote, each opposition party concentrates on its electoral base—the public sector labor unions for the JSP, the faithful for the Komeito, and so forth.

For conservatives, the race within a district focuses on images, local organization, and the "bag" of money (the trio of *kamban, jiban, kaban*) crisply described by Nathaniel Thayer in *How the Conservatives Rule Japan*. When money to nurture the candidates' organizations became noteworthy, the press would report "real bullets" flying around. Issues matter, but you wouldn't know it from candidate behavior, which focuses on mustering the organization. The media explore issues, but there are few debates among party leaders, much less among candidates themselves.

With few exceptions, LDP candidates are political parties unto themselves. Most have a *koenkai* (support organization) as the core of their votes and the motor of the campaign. In the big cities a few LDP candidates pound the pavement looking for individual votes, but such cases are rare. The *koenkai* devours money for such local concerns as weddings, funerals, parties, festivals, and pet causes. In many respects Japanese politics lacks popular participation; but politicians argue, not without reason, that in one respect politics suffers from excessive responsiveness: attention to the *koenkai*. Only national leaders can readily disregard its wishes. The focus of constituent services is on the *koenkai* rather than on the district as a whole, from which the candidate needs only a small minority of the vote to get elected.

Competition among conservatives fuels an insatiable need for campaign funds. Diet members from different LDP factions—persons to whom no scandal attaches—have said frankly that everyone violates spending limits, which are ridiculously low. (Some young Diet members have said so publicly.) The public knows it and often believes, as casual interlocutors have said, that "all politicians are dishonest." They are not, but politicians are increasingly viewed with disdain, a matter that bothers some but to which others seem indifferent. As Gerald L. Curtis, cited earlier, pointed out, scandals spark periodic reforms of campaign spending laws, but each new reform is as unrealistic as the last, spawning new evasions. Those evasions have fostered the growth of soft money, the kind that can have a hard-edged payoff.

The factions are coalitions of the members. The factions help members get elected, mostly by funneling funds to candidates from the faction. In Tokyo, the faction's role is to secure advancement to the cabinet for senior members and, if possible, to the prime ministership for the faction leader. Less and less are the Liberal Democrats a party; more and more the LDP has become a coalition of coalitions. Parliamentary discipline, supposedly a hallmark of parliamentary systems, has become more apparent than real, as in the case of the proposal for electoral reform that brought down the Kaifu cabinet. The electoral system is a cause of the policy gridlock that afflicts the government, of frequent changes of prime ministers, and of even more frequent changes of cabinet, a sort of "ticket punching" for senior politicians.

The Diet is not a place for debate, despite the question period, in which the prime minister and cabinet respond to queries. Committees discuss legislation only little because of the opposition practice of walking out of deliberations to delay or prevent passage of uncongenial legislation. There is a Kabuki-like ritual to those walkouts, covered all too seriously by the press. Sometimes backroom discussions with the opposition, out of public sight and involving trade-offs, may produce agreement to let a bill, or a modified version, go forward without much delay.

In the question period, there is little of the penetrating debate that sometimes marks the British House of Commons, as a senior LDP leader complained to me. The handlers, in this case the bureaucracy, provide government responders, from the prime minister on down, with bland and opaque replies. The style is for the opposition to repeat the same question in different words, sometimes over and over, in hopes of driving a wedge between the first answer of the minister and his later remarks. The bureaucracy serves up standardized responses, in essence saying the same thing, and hopes the minister will not stray from the script. Some time ago, a conservative leader, an acquaintance of a few years, said that the functioning of the Diet and the political system is a "threat to Japanese democracy." He feared the non-performance of the Diet was eroding public confidence in the institutions of democracy, a judgment confirmed by the low voting rate in the last Upper House election.

As a young Diet member explained in frustration, the average members have little time for policy; their days are spent in fund raising, except for the hours in session. The electoral system strengthens factionalism because demands for money are so great that most candidates must depend on the faction for substantial funding. Factions are by no means alien to the West. But as Professor Kyogoku explains, factionalism in Japan is more deeply rooted in, among other things, the strong group identities developed among feudal clans and peasant communities alike during two and a half centuries of Tokugawa rule.

For years, Japanese and foreign observers studied the LDP's many-layered Policy Affairs Research Council (*seichokai*) looking for keys to how the LDP makes policy. The inquiry may have been a waste of time. Factionalism has come to impede policy discussion even within the LDP. With some unhappiness a former cabinet minister told me, "We are reluctant these days to discuss policy with other LDP factions; we discuss issues frankly only among our own faction."

In the March 23, 1992, *Nihon Keizai*, Japan's analogue to the *Wall Street Journal*, political commentator Keiichiro Nakamura looked back with nostalgia. Today's factional rivalries, he wrote, are "private spats" compared to the clashes between Tanaka and Fukuda and between Miki and Sato (all prime ministers) that featured "national themes as the points of contention." If you can't debate policy with the opposition in the Diet, and you can't freely debate policy even within party councils, no wonder there is gridlock.

The demand for funds fostered by the electoral system spawned "tribes" (*zoku*), informal groups of LDP backbenchers, cutting across factions. Each *zoku* gets financing largely from a single economic sector, the construction, transportation, and agricultural sectors being three principal tribes. Factions tolerate *zoku* because they are a source of contributions. *Zoku* came into their own in the 1970s and operate as intraparty lobbies to encourage legislation and, most important, to discourage actions that might interfere with their sectors, as in the liberalization of the construction sector, where costs are inflated by bid rigging (*dango*). Nothing in America is directly analogous to the *zoku*, but influence buying through political contributions to the legislative and executive branch by industries such as the S&Ls has been amply documented.

Take an example of policy stagnation. Japanese lobbyists accuse the United States of agricultural rape, of forcing Japan to liberalize the rice market. An agricultural magazine raises the specter of the weevil monster and shows Japanese in danger from pesticides on American rice; the article does not suggest standards but demands, in language reminiscent of the "Japanese snow is different" flap over foreign-made skis, the exclusion of foreign rice. That insular approach to foreign products has not been unusual; not only were skis from abroad proscribed for a time because they were allegedly unsuitable to Japanese snow, but so were foreign-made baseball bats, which were deemed somehow inappropriate for the Japanese. It is, however, a sign of change that those arguments met with ridicule from many Japanese and the barriers were eventually dropped.

Indeed, Japan's general policy towards agricultural imports is now quite liberal, as is reflected in the enormous imports of foodstuffs from the United States, and it is much in Japan's interest to help break the GATT deadlock in agricultural products that is largely due to European protectionism. For Japan, rice is the sticking point, and Europeans have used Tokyo's rice-calcitrance as one excuse for not liberalizing agricultural policy. Polls show a majority of Japanese favor at least partial liberalization. In the words of a train conductor who brought up the subject, "if we can export all those cars to your country, we can surely buy some of your rice." Industrial users (crackers, sushi chains, etc.) want to buy foreign rice. Growers of premium rice expect liberalization to increase profits. Senior ruling party figures have long hinted publicly at liberalization. In private, they are explicit. So why can't the government act?

One answer is found in a Japanese joke. "There is one bureaucrat for every farmer." The LDP is hostage to pressure groups—in this case, Nokyo, a nongovernmental bureaucracy that controls the agricultural cooperatives. For the most part, the bureaucrats are not farmers, and are often resented by real farmers. They have a vested interest in the power that control over agricultural pricing and production gives them, and they have a near stranglehold on agricultural policy. Each time the government has nudged up to a modest liberalization in rice, Nokyo squeezes its "tribe" of LDP members and the government backs away.

Bureaucratization

Japan's domestic goals were achieved in stunning fashion. Now, at a stroke, long-standing international goals have also been reached with the demise of the Soviet Union. In the words of a seasoned Japanese observer: "The bureaucracy was well suited to running the national train down a straight track, towards prosperity, in the comfort of the security relationship with the United States. The train has arrived. From here, several tracks are open, but the bureaucracy cannot throw the switches. Only the elected political leadership can do that and they appear incapable."

Much of the élan that characterized the elite bureaucracy is gone. For example, the Finance Ministry is the home of the best and the brightest. But when the ministry's cozy (and unwritten) regulatory relationship with Nomura, Nikko, and other securities firms led to scandal in the financial markets, the ministry did not act on the obvious conclusion that an independent regulatory body was necessary to restore confidence in the markets. The great security houses, with the sanction of the ministry, had secretly covered losses of major investors, including a prominent gangster, while the small investors took a bath. That hurt the confidence of the public (not to mention that of international investors) in the markets, one cause of the freefall in the Nikkei index.

A successful Japanese investor, who left the Japanese market for a time, diagnosed the problem in private. "The U.S. has financial scandals, but your markets are reasonably transparent, and your SEC gives the investor some confidence that markets are not rigged. The average Japanese investor has no such surety and has reason to be suspicious. We are not so well protected as the U.S. investor; Japan needs something like the SEC."

The press and some leading LDP politicians favored an independent body, but the Finance Ministry and the securities industry resisted the idea and produced for cosmetic change a regulatory group controlled by the ministry. Turf was preserved and the interests of citizen investors sacrificed at a cost to the economy. Regulatory inaction kept alive investor concerns about the reliability of the market and contributed to the slide; before the recent partial recovery, the market lost 60 percent of its value in a two-year period.

Bureaucratization is also reflected in over-centralization of administration and authority in Tokyo. To illustrate the unresponsiveness of the central bureaucracy, Governor Hosokawa has cited how it took several years to get Tokyo to agree to a Kumamoto prefecture decision to change the location of a bus stop. Though, as central government figures will point out, local officials are skilled in extracting projects from Tokyo, most resent the pilgrimages to Kasumigaseki and Nagata-cho (the respective seats of the bureaucracy and the LDP in Tokyo) for decisions and resources they believe should be the province of local government.

There is no sentiment favoring a federal system, but regional consciousness is deeply rooted. The call for decentralization, for devolution of powers to provinces and cities, and for more control over budgets and taxation is heard everywhere outside Tokyo, no longer just in Osaka and Nagoya, the traditional homes of sentiment for greater regional control over local destinies. For example, an innovative idea comes from a one-time backwater, the Tohoku region of northern Japan, now modernizing with the extension of the "bullet train" northward. The LDP leadership in the six provinces suggests a "super province," combining administration of the six into one, to give the region more clout. I have listened to politicians and journalists, not only from Tohoku but from the southernmost main island, Kyushu, advocate "super provinces."

Interviews generally revealed a belief that local politicians and bureaucrats are closer to the people, more responsive to their public, than the national bureaucracy and political leadership. That is because the voter often shows no compunction in local elections about choosing socialist, independent, or opposition coalition governors, mayors, and local assemblies, particularly in urban areas. In local elections there is often a real choice between LDP candidates and those who run against them.

In an interview, a leading regional journalist, concerned about the erosion of democratic values he sees in younger Japanese, went beyond regional concerns to suggest that decentralization is critical to restoring popular participation and interest in Japan's democratic institutions. There is support for his view in the emergence of a new "grassroots" phenomenon, nonpartisan civic slates driven by women's groups interested in consumer issues and the environment. Now active in ten prefectures, their low-cost, volunteer, door-to-door campaigns have the potential to open up politics; for example, in the last local elections in Kanagawa prefecture (where Yokohama is located), a citizens' coalition elected fifty-seven women to various local assemblies, roughly double the number the movement had elected four years earlier.

Decentralization might ease the accounting of central government. Regional governments have generally run a modest surplus—while the central government ran a deficit until recently and will now run one again in response to the recession. A proper distribution of fiscal responsibilities could allow more easily for generous central government investment in infrastructure, which the people need. Like so many reform questions, decentralization is going nowhere today, despite the customary blue-ribbon study groups. In Tokyo, businessmen and politicians suggest decentralization's time will come, though not immediately. Decentralization has not been at the top of the public's wish list (one recent poll suggests that about 19 percent of the public give administrative reform priority). But local elites are tired of bowing to Tokyo politicians and bureaucrats in the search for resources and will keep up the pressure.

Japanese Leadership

The conventional wisdom among Euro-American observers, and among many Japanese as well, has been that prime ministers lack leadership. That judgment often reflects insistence on defining leadership in Western terms—as a charismatic or, as in the case of Truman, a take-charge type. In those terms only Yoshida, Kishi, and Yasuhiro Nakasone fit the bill. Yoshida was characterized as "one man" rule (only partly true; Yoshida had able advisors and, much of the time, General MacArthur in the background), Kishi was in visible charge, and Nakasone has been a commanding presence wherever he goes.

The story is different if leadership is defined in terms of Japan's political culture, with its emphasis after 1960 on building consensus, defined as agreement on a course of action or, as it has more and more come to be, tacit acceptance of that course. Until recently, most prime ministers came to power with defined policy agendas, which played a role in their selection and which they sought to achieve. Kishi's experience is instructive. Like his friend Richard Nixon, Kishi had a remarkable grasp of international interests, but was less successful at home. Despite having been purged by the occupation for wartime service as a civilian official of government, Kishi wanted alliance with the U.S., even as he sought full restoration of Japan's sovereignty, restricted by the 1952 Security Treaty, which permitted the U.S. to intervene in Japan's domestic affairs. He meshed those goals in the 1960 revision of the Security Treaty, which proved a most durable instrument for cooperation and a monument to Kishi's statesmanship.

Domestically, however, Kishi failed to understand the temper of the people and sentiment within his own party against tampering with so many reforms of the occupation. When Ikeda took over in 1960, he abandoned the "reverse course" for a domestic agenda aimed at prosperity.

Eisaku Sato, Ikeda's rival and successor in 1965, was also a consensus seeker. Sato, however, had a risky international agenda, which many saw as an impossible dream, of combining the reversion of Okinawa to Japanese sovereignty with the depoliticization of the security relationship with the United States.

The Pentagon had huge reservations about giving up its less-than-happy stewardship of Okinawa. There was much sparring. Eventually, the Japanese came up with a specific plan for reversion. Its central feature maintained U.S. bases on Okinawa after reversion but under the same conditions as those on the mainland. Japan would obtain full sovereignty, reversion at the "homeland level" (*hondo nami*) rather than the "partial sovereignty" advocated by some U.S strategists. The Security Treaty, up for possible review, would be left intact. The principal architect, Kiichi Aichi, shortly to become foreign minister, "unofficially" provided the contents of the plan to the United States. Discussions began that led to President Nixon's agreement with Sato in late 1969 to return Okinawa without restrictions on Japanese sovereignty and leave the Security Treaty intact. The bargain was very popular, giving the LDP its largest Lower House election victory.

The talks were facilitated by Kishi's private visit to Nixon in early 1969 and by the labors of Japanese and American diplomats, notably U. Alexis Johnson and the late Richard L. Sneider for the Americans. Nixon's decision fits on any list of the ten most important Cold War decisions; it did what nothing else could: It ensured Japanese public acceptance of the security relationship, the cornerstone of containment in the Pacific. In domestic affairs the country followed Ikeda's growth policies, but the unhappy record of trade disputes with the United States began with Sato, whose "best efforts" to impose "voluntary" restraints on textile exports were stymied by textile interests in the LDP. Nixon felt a promise had been broken and retaliated with the "Nixon shocks"—not giving Japan notice of the opening to China or of his decision to devalue the dollar.

Most prime ministers who followed had agendas that played a role in their selection. Takeo Miki (1974–76) sought, with limited success, to clean up corruption after Kakuei Tanaka (1972–74). The term of Takeo Fukuda (1976–78) was cut short by rivals, but he restored fiscal discipline and economic growth after the first OPEC oil price shocks. Death cut short Ohira's term (1978–80), but before he died he revised Japan's international agenda and made Japan a major provider of economic assistance. By objective standards, both exerted leadership. In contrast, Ohira's agenda-less successor, Zenko Suzuki (1980–82), foundered without a trace.

Nakasone (1982–87) was the last effective prime minister—not that everything went well; his administration was called the "Tanakasone" government by critics who deplored his reliance on Tanaka. Nakasone, however, had his own agenda. He privatized state enterprises and, above all, his presence and his relationship with U.S. President Ronald Reagan gave Japan an international image and voice more commensurate with its economic power. Others, Fukuda and Ohira, possessed excellent reputations abroad. But Nakasone put Japan on the map in a new way, made it prominent as well as important. For a brief moment, he also made the prime ministry a place where personal popularity as well as party strength was a source of power.

Has the Prime Ministry Become Powerless?

The weakening of the prime minister's office became apparent during the prime ministership of Takeshita, who seized control of the Tanaka faction after the latter's stroke. Renowned for political smarts, Takeshita succeeded Nakasone in 1988 with an explicit agenda: to regularize government revenues through a value added–style tax, which he pushed through the Diet, and to control trade frictions with the United States.

Even with time the latter might have been impossible, but Takeshita's cabinet was undermined by the Recruit scandal. Takeshita, after resigning in 1989, made an uncharacteristic error: He imposed a party nonentity, Sosuke Uno, as prime minister, to lead a government ruled from behind the scenes by Takeshita. Uno lasted two months. The leadership, buffeted by the loss of the LDP's Upper House majority, next looked for an attractive, younger face, untouched by scandal. They found him in Toshiki Kaifu, a leader in the party's smallest faction. A gifted speaker, Kaifu seemed a breath of fresh air and developed great personal popularity, which he retains today, out of office.

The Persian Gulf war was Kaifu's great headache. Rivals tried to push him out because of "lack of leadership." Kaifu won a general election victory, and his rivals found that ousting him was not so simple. Kaifu survived the first attempts, but never controlled the party or the bureaucracy. He depended on the Takeshita faction, with whom relations were uneasy, for survival. It was not foreign policy but Kaifu's desire to reform the Lower House electoral system along lines recommended by a select commission that brought him down. When he sought to dissolve the Diet to stand for election on that issue, the party leadership refused. Unable to exercise his constitutional prerogative of dissolving the Diet, Kaifu resigned. His successor, Kiichi Miyazawa, said Japan needed an experienced prime minister with a strong economic and international background who could lead, particularly in the international arena.

Miyazawa had bad luck from the start, particularly in President George Bush's decision to postpone his visit from November of 1991 to the first of 1992 and turn the visit from an exercise in statecraft, in which the two could lay a framework for a post–Cold War relationship, into a poorly thought-out trade mission. The recession also hurt—all the more because it was unpredicted; economists erroneously foresaw a future that looked much like their present, a leveling of growth but no recession.

New scandals and the image that he, too, could not move without approval from the Takeshita faction, brought offhand predictions that Miyazawa would not last the year. Instead, Miyazawa's stock rebounded with passage of the bill to authorize limited participation in U.N. peacekeeping activities and the LDP's relative success in the subsequent Upper House elections. His respite was short-lived. The latest scandal involving Sagawa Kyubin, a Japanese version of the United Parcel Service, forced the party's reigning *eminence gris*, Shin Kanemaru, to resign from the Diet. Though Miyazawa is not involved, other senior LDP figures are implicated. The party is in disarray.

The question persists: Even allowing for Japan's decision-making style, has the prime ministry become "emperorized," a relatively powerless post to which leaders aspire for years only to face retirement in short order? To that question there is no categorical answer. In a reform climate, a prime minister will recover prestige and authority. When democratic institutions atrophy, the prime ministry will not escape and is likely to become the permanent plaything of behind-the-scenes power brokers, called *kuromaku* for their resemblance to the black-clad puppeteers of the Bunraku theater.

The School for Scandal

The corruption of the 1950s was memorialized in Akira Kurosawa's film *Warui Yatsu Hodo Yoku Nemuro* (in English, *The Bad Sleep Well*—literally, the more evil you are, the better you sleep). A manual of style for the corrupt, it is the blackest of Japanese *film noir*, wildly funny and deeply pessimistic. In the film, company officials commit suicide to avoid implicating the boss, who relies on gangsters and who coldly destroys his daughter's sanity to protect his patron, an unheard presence on the other end of the telephone who is presumably a senior politician.

"The Problem Is Tanaka"

In the late 1960s, the conservatives were again shaken, for the first time in a number of years, by several scandals, largely unremembered except for the imaginative name, the "black mist" (*kuroi kiri*), which the press gave them.

In the wake of the "black mist," I made the rounds of LDP figures to ask how much the scandal would affect the LDP and what the party would do. Two conversations stand out in memory. The first was with Kakuei Tanaka himself, who in friendly fashion dismissed the "black mist" as a minor affair—which it was, compared with what followed—and said the LDP was in good shape. Another LDP leader, now long dead, warmed to the issue. Some corruption is inevitable, he said, but things are out of hand. "The problem is Tanaka" (who was then secretary general of the LDP, in charge of the party purse). If unchecked, Tanaka will ruin politics, he suggested. At the time, I partly discounted the remarks as sour grapes coming from an elitist rival.

In fact, many observers saw hope in Tanaka's rise. For example, a knowledgeable scholar, Haruhiku Fukui, praised Tanaka as a "populist" (see *Party in Power*). Here was a self-made politician who had not gone to the right schools, who might broaden Japanese democracy, which was weighed down by bureaucratic elitism. Today, the view is different. Political observers and many conservative politicians attribute the decay in politics to unbridled growth in corruption under Tanaka. From 1969 to 1972 Tanaka, with ample access to shadowy funds from the construction sector then controlled by construction magnate and Tanaka confidant Kenji Osano, increased the size of his faction. In 1972, Tanaka became prime minister. After he was forced out by scandal in 1974, the Lockheed bribery was exposed in the course of a congressional investigation in the United States. Boxes of cash had been conveyed to Tanaka through the late Yoshio Kodama, a wartime firebrand who became a godfather figure for both the far Right and the *yakuza*. Eventually, Tanaka was convicted in a Japanese court.

The Tanaka experience runs counter to the conventional western leadership paradigm. In those terms, Tanaka was a strong, visible leader, but what did he do for Japan? Tanaka's agenda has been described as "power for the sake of power," as only thinking of expanding his faction. As a Japanese newsman pointed out, Tanaka is called a political genius; but each time he controlled electoral strategy, the LDP did not do well, though his faction did splendidly. Tanaka's Huey Long–style populism had little content. He seems to have had no policy agenda except to stimulate the construction sector through nationwide public works. After indictment, until his stroke in 1985, Tanaka unmade cabinets, getting revenge on his successor, Takeo Miki, who wanted to reform politics and refused to stop Tanaka's prosecution. Later, he cut short his old enemy, Fukuda. Tanaka left a legacy of political gridlock:

- He dramatically increased the amount of money needed by conservatives to gain election, all too frequently with no questions asked. Those who did not belong to Tanaka's faction struggled to raise similar amounts of soft money in order to compete.

- He created a super-faction, today the Takeshita faction, so large that no prime minister could stay in office and no new policy could be undertaken without its approval.

- He undermined the importance of policy agendas in the intra-party contention over who should be prime minister.

The 1980s—Scandals Go Big Time

When the yen rose after the 1985 Plaza Accord, the Bank of Japan lowered the discount rate to levels unprecedented for a growing economy, to 2.5 percent at the lowest point. Cheap money helped industry finance the adjustment by sharply lowering the cost of capital far below that of capital in the rest of the world. On one occasion, a Toyota bond offering went at 1.4 percent, a negative interest rate of the sort the International Monetary Fund condemns in developing countries.

Easy money had other effects, such as fostering speculation in land and stocks. Politicians found the "bubble" a generous source of contributions. Even businesses, once models of prudence, became hooked, as *zaiteku* (high-tech finance) became the vogue. Why else would Matsushita—a world leader in electronics, skilled in making profitable things—stray from its strength to venture into a non-bank financial institution? Much as on Wall Street during the leveraged buy-outs mania, a powerful lobby justified the madness, explaining the phenomenal growth in land prices and the Nikkei index as evidence of Japan's prowess. The price-earnings ratio, they said, was irrelevant to a Japan that operated by superior rules. In a reminder of shared inadequacies, Japanese apologists praised the bubble in language reminiscent of Michael Milken's "creating value."

The exposure of the first great scandal of the 1980s began to deflate the bubble. Recruit Cosmos began as an employment agency, but found land enticing and built a speculative empire. Its founder, Hiromasa Ezoe, moved from outsider to confidant of politicians, and into the Keizaidoyukai, an elite business group that historically offered a fresher perspective than the more bureaucratic Keidanren (the Federation of Japanese Economic Organizations) at the pinnacle of business. Recruit provided a new stock issue—before listing it—to politicians, including some from opposition parties, as a supposedly guaranteed quick profit. The exposure of that scheme led to prosecutions. Only one prominent LDP politician stands accused of criminal activity, but several—including Nakasone—resigned from the party to atone for connections with the affair (they have since returned). The Recruit affair represented a power play gone wrong, an effort to shift the balance within the business and political establishment.

Prudent establishment figures had warned early on about disaster lurking in the bubble (I recall Keidanren officials citing danger), but nothing happened. Recruit had a sobering effect on economic management. Under new leadership, the Bank of Japan began raising the discount rate, steadily tightening credit. Some politicians blamed the bank for the recession, but greed (theirs included) had built the bubble to a point at which lancing could only produce pain. Other scandals followed. The latest, Sagawa Kyubin, is particularly important for its confirmation of *yakuza* influence in politics. Involving huge amounts of questionable transactions by the express company, some touching the political world, the affair surfaced before the July 1992 Upper House elections. The prosecutors, however, did not reveal significant information about its political dimension until after those elections.

Sagawa Kyubin was widely known for its use of *yakuza* to settle traffic accidents and for the use of political connections to bend government rules to expedite deliveries. Many people looked the other way at such things until the trial of Sagawa's ex-president brought scandal into the heart of the ruling party and forced Japanese to look into the mirror of their politics. The first revelations were about the ex-governor of Niigata, the home prefecture of former prime minister Tanaka. The governor is charged with receiving a large illegal contribution from Sagawa Kyubin, reportedly tied to a scheme to corner the freight and express market to China (imagine a parcel route with a billion people) through facilities at Niigata City on the Japan Sea.

The most prominent casualty was the Takeshita faction's titular leader, former LDP vice-president Shin Kanemaru. The arbiter of politics (he reputedly chose Kaifu and anointed Miyazawa for the prime ministership), Kanemaru admitted to receiving $4 million in cash—carried away in shopping carts, according to testimony—for the campaigns of faction members. He resigned the party post and offered to resign the faction leadership. Three factors lifted the scandal out of the ordinary and fueled public ire: the intimate connection with the *yakuza*, Kanemaru's bizarre tug of war with his prosecutors, and the refusal of his faction—which feared breakup—to let him resign, the norm in such matters.

To avoid questioning by prosecutors, for seventeen days Kanemaru refused to leave his home, which was surrounded by reporters and TV cameras day and night. Finally, he pled guilty in writing to violating campaign limits (the specified fine is $1,600), prompting public ridicule. In turn, the prosecutors gave up on questioning him. The unusual plea bargain sparked public criticism of the prosecutors and Kanemaru for putting politicians above the law. That anger is reportedly shared by many in the prosecutor's office who believe political pressure had prevented their office from pursuing the affair: The express service also provided $16 million dollars in contributions to about ten national politicians. (The *Sankei* newspaper quotes a Sagawa official describing politicians who took money as "tame cats.") More revelations have followed.

What Happened to the Common Good?

Whom can a Japanese trust when a prestigious bank and one of the world's premier electronics firms loan a restaurant owner a total of a billion dollars for speculation, on tips derived from astrologers, in a stock market sinking like a rock? It is little comfort that General Motors threw away almost half that sum on a car dealer's nonexistent inventory; that sort of incompetence is not supposed to occur in Japan. Scandals have called into question the competence of the establishment, politicians, business, and the bureaucracy. Sometimes, as in the case of Sagawa Kyubin, they raise the issue of systemic corruption.

Even before Sagawa people knew something was wrong, though discontent has been unfocused. In magnitude and frequency, the scandals exceed tolerable limits, as sensible politicians themselves say. Before the recession got the public's attention, in two spring 1992 surveys 40 percent of the public placed political reform at the top of their national wish list, and the latest surveys suggest that public interest in political reform is returning.

The public has become disturbed about unfairness. The newly rich *narikin* with big cars, lavish houses, private museums, and ostentatious lifestyles are evidence that the sweat of the average Japanese benefits the few. Japanese are embarrassed by the *narikin*, who buy up houses by the dozen in Hawaii and turn golf courses into paper gold. The Bentleys and Mercedes with darkened windows that line the side streets of Roppongi—an "in" place for the after-hours crowd—are seen as the product of dubious money, a reproach to the work ethic. Some of the newly rich are gangsters. There is hardly a new golf course, Japanese say, that does not have gangland involvement, and the *yakuza* have internationalized into resorts and rackets in Southeast Asia and the South Pacific. Though the numbers of *yakuza* have fallen, according to police statistics, wealth from the bubble has brought greater power. Each day seems to bring a new scandal. The latest touches the United States: The head of Ito-Yokado, the owner of the 7-11 chain, has just resigned because of publicity over his gangland connections.

It is disturbing to a sympathetic foreigner to ask casually in a public place about the *yakuza* and watch an ordinary Japanese, speaking freely about all manner of things, lean forward and lower his voice before answering. The *Mainichi* newspaper's brilliant investigative series relates the little stories: an accident with a gangster's car that becomes a financial nightmare for an ordinary family, a reporter on the series who gets a call, laden with unspoken menace, from a gang leader—at home, on the reporter's unlisted number. The *Mainichi* suggests the roots of underworld power lie in "surface" society, where respectable people, businessmen and politicians, sometimes rely on the "dark" world for services.

The Sagawa Kyubin affair and hidden rebates to *yakuza* from leading security firms confirm that view. The rebates from security houses to a leading gangster, the late Susumu Ishii, were prominent in the scandals that helped drive down the financial markets. Kanemaru used the then president of Sagawa Kyubin to get that same Mr. Ishii to intercede with a right-wing group to "persuade" them to stop publicly embarrassing Takeshita, then on the eve of becoming prime minister. The return favors included Sagawa's guarantee on large loans to Ishii and Takeshita's calling at the house of former prime minister Tanaka to apologize for usurping the faction's leadership. (The press reports that Tanaka refused to see him.) As a Japanese said, "We knew a little of this went on, but now we have to wonder who's in charge." The blatant reliance on the underworld has shaken the LDP in general and the Takeshita faction in particular and has even prompted faint stirrings among the business establishment in favor of real political reform.

Growing concern about the *yakuza* has inspired a police campaign to push them back into their traditional, demarcated rackets. Some underlings are trying to make a break, going into rehab programs, but the trickle has not become a flood. (The press reports a plea to police of one would-be retiree from the *yakuza*, "How can I get out? They want me either to pay or cut off my little finger.") The police are armed with new legislation against criminal conspiracy, but the law is deficient in one respect. The route to a criminal's power is through his wallet. In the skeptical view, the lack of a clear-cut forfeiture-of-assets provision in the new law is a result of embarrassment—laundered *yakuza* funds may have wound up in respectable endeavors. Gang finances, however, have taken a hit from the lancing of the bubble. The *Mainichi* carries convincing interviews with gangsters saying how difficult it is to turn a buck. It is hard to believe that those in the establishment who pressed for monetary prudence did not have that result in mind.

Even movies are changing. With few exceptions, films have purveyed a phony view of the *yakuza* as comic figures or idealistic rogues. That distortion has played at the box office in Japan, just as idealization of the Mafia has sold in the United States (*yakuza* connections with the entertainment world were a factor). In the late 1980s, Juzo Itami's *Taxing Woman II* broke the mold, acidly portraying links among crime, conservative politicians, and business. Recent films, including Itami's *Mimbo*, put gangland behavior under the microscope. The *yakuza* saw a threat in such films and conducted a drive-by stabbing of Itami. They cut "slowly," a defiant Itami said to the *New York Times*, aiming to maim, to intimidate. In his book, Professor Kyogoku speaks of historical patterns of popular indignation against "upstarts," those who profit illicitly from the system, that have forced change in Japan. One hopes, but cannot be sure, that gangster intimidation will kindle popular anger lying beneath the surface enough to break *yakuza* power.

The Road to Reform

The cumulative weight of scandal has a corroding effect, not only on politics but on the Japanese people's vision of themselves as a country of probity, hard work, and unostentatious living. Prospects for reform exist but have run up against popular apathy, bred of the lack of choice and a certain smugness that results from Japan's economic success. That apathy, coupled with a relative absence of organized citizen activity, leads to a conclusion that one cause of political malaise is a lack of popular participation in politics.

Business and agricultural lobbies exist, of course, and so do unions, which are finding the opposition parties to which they are linked to be increasingly irrelevant. But public interest groups (what we sometimes call nongovernmental organizations) have little strength on the national level, though their influence is demonstrably growing in various localities.

The nascent women's movement has yet to find sustained political expression, though women are driving many of the "grassroots" movements (*kusa-no-ne undo*), such as consumer cooperatives and much of a growing environmental movement. In discussing Japanese youth, an American professor tells his students to read F. Scott Fitzgerald's *The Great Gatsby*. The young are no longer politically active. Many Japanese are sensibly interested in the environment, and environmental organizations are beginning to gather strength, with some early but still inconclusive success in such matters as cleaning up water sources, a major danger to Japan's environment.

The consumer movement has not advanced much beyond the stage of buying cooperatives, which have had success in using buying power to ensure quality and purity in foodstuffs and in promoting environmentally safe products. The movement has not focused on anti-competitive practices and their cost to consumers, though polls indicate average Japanese recognize the problem. In the words of a taxi driver, "What I buy costs three times more than what you buy in your country because of a distribution system no one understands and where profits go to unknown people."

The present condition is not permanent. Grassroots movements have historical precedents. In feudal times they produced local explosions against the exactions of rulers. In Meiji, the first political parties were formed in the provinces. In the postwar era, student idealism contributed to democracy before radicals compromised the movement, ending student involvement in politics. Private-sector labor unions, until recently, had success in getting companies to raise the workers' standard of living. The Japanese versions of PTAs, Rotary and Lions Clubs, Soroptimists, and other organizations, engage in community service. What may be missing is a connection between community and national issues. Today, grassroots groups are on the rise. They do not as yet, however, press a claim on national politics.

The House of Cards (Electoral Reform)

The electoral system itself—the legitimate vehicle for change—is a prime cause of corruption because of rapacious demands it creates for campaign finance. The direct route to reform lies in the Lower House electoral system. It is thought that major reform in the way Lower House members are elected would lead to real change, shaking up the parties and providing the voter with genuine options. Even within the LDP itself—which does not want for dedicated members who feel trapped by the system—there is great sentiment for making politics more effective. So why hasn't reform happened?

From its beginnings in 1955, the LDP, as the largest party, wanted a British system of single-member districts, which would provide, given historical voting percentages, an ample majority. First made by Prime Minister Ichiro Hatoyama in furtherance of the "reverse course," the proposal was supposed to bring about the two-thirds majority necessary to change the constitution. The "Hatoyama-mander," as Japanese critics called it, went nowhere. For its part, the opposition has always supported proportional representation because it might produce, given usual voting rates, an opposition majority. A straight proportional system would also likely produce, given a fragmented opposition, the ills of the French Third Republic: frequent, dizzying changes of government, a fatal flaw.

The blue-ribbon commission referred to earlier brought together respected figures from parties, the media, the academic world, and business, among others. It was driven forward by a senior LDP leader, Tsutomu Hata, who was interested in rescuing politics from its low estate. The commission reached a practical conclusion, attuned to Japanese reality: elect the Lower House through a combination of single-member districts and proportional representation. Under current voting rates, the proposed system would initially produce results roughly similar to the existing pattern. No party would be disadvantaged per se. But the mixed system proposed by the blue-ribbon commission would push the noncommunist opposition toward coalescence and would shift the race from ever more costly competition among conservatives to a competition between conservatives and their restructured opposition, providing the electorate with real alternatives.[5]

Forward-looking LDP members favored the compromise and Kaifu put his prime ministry on the line for it. The LDP would not be hurt; under some scenarios it might even slightly increase its seats in the first elections under the new system. Individuals, however, would lose seats. Second-echelon long-timers were particularly fearful. Most important, faction leaders were reluctant, not because it would end factions—something that is not going to happen in Japan—but because the new system would shake things up.

Another proposal, allowing the citizen to vote for as many candidates as there are seats in his or her district, would force candidates to reach out beyond their personal support organizations, reducing the *koenkai*'s power, because winners would need a majority of the district's votes. The proposal, however, would not decrease competition among conservatives or the cost of campaigns. In short, it would not promote political choice.

There is yet another plan, perhaps the most likely vehicle for reform, should it come soon. Like the select commission proposal, it represents a compromise between the positions of the LDP and the opposition. The idea is to elect the Lower House entirely from single-member districts and the Upper House entirely by proportional representation. That could initially preserve the equities of existing parties, reduce the costs of campaigning and the power of the *koenkai*, and retain the Upper House's role as a check on the "tyranny of the majority" in such matters as constitutional reform. In the wake of Sagawa Kyubin, Prime Minister Miyazawa has begun to talk about reopening the question of basic reforms.

The immediate outlook is for only a modest reallocation to meet court-mandated redistricting. The minimum standard set by the court is generous: The worth of a vote in a district should not exceed three times that of a vote in any other district. A few LDP members—careless of all legitimacy—voiced the thought of going ahead without redistricting. (One was quoted as saying the Diet should resist the judiciary's "interference in the separation of powers.") But as sensible members argued, ignoring the court would produce constitutional crisis. Discussions are underway about formulas to take away seats from less-populous areas and add them to more-populous districts, for example to take away ten seats and add nine, which would reduce the disparity to a 2.7:1 ratio. While important, redistricting is not the same as electoral system reform—but it could have the consequence of nudging reform forward.

The "Great Restructuring"

The "great restructuring" (*seiji saihensei*) is Japanese politics' snake that will not die. The thought is for the LDP and the noncommunist opposition to break apart and regroup into a center- to moderate-left party and a party of traditional conservatives. The argument has always gone roughly like this: One-party rule is decaying, and circumstances require alternation in power, which cannot be achieved by the traditional opposition.

In fact, the only example of a great restructuring in the postwar period took the opposite course. In 1955, under pressure from business, the two conservative parties, led respectively by Yoshida and Hatoyama, joined to form the LDP in order to prevent the Left, then much stronger, from winning another election.

By the late 1960s, straight-line projections of a declining LDP vote persuaded many Japanese and foreign observers to predict that the opposition would come to power by the early to mid 1970s, unless moderate conservatives from the LDP split the party and drew to them moderate socialists and the smaller opposition parties to form a new center-left group, to provide a true two-party system capable of alternation in power. The Keidanren seems to have flirted with the notion, but business support, essential to financing new parties, never materialized. In the 1970s the New Liberals tried, but they were too few and business wouldn't buy. Demographic change and the willingness of the LDP to adjust policy to meet voter aspirations put a halt to such speculation.

The 1980s spawned a new version. Restructuring would come from realignment of the opposition in which non-ideological Socialists and the small DSP and maybe the Komeito would unite. That scenario, as a Japanese newsman observed, offered an incentive for an LDP split, because the table of coalition government would be set if a strong bloc of conservatives came across to join with moderate opposition. The new party would have numbers to form a government, in which the LDP component, by virtue of experience, would have a major leadership role.

The opposition never realigned, so the proposition remains untested. The Upper House election, marked by Socialist decline and the collapse of the Rengo option, has revived speculation about opposition restructuring. On the conservative side, Governor Hosokawa aims to reactivate the scenario of a new, moderate reformist party that attracts like-minded politicians from the LDP.

Be that as it may, a senior LDP figure who has not lost his sense of humor suggested early in 1992 that the way things were, the only way to achieve a "great restructuring" would be for the huge Takeshita faction to declare itself a political party. In that election the Takeshita faction increased its share of Upper House seats relative to the other factions. Its leadership frankly aimed at doing the same in the coming Lower House elections, with the evident goal of obtaining an absolute majority of the LDP Diet seats, making the other factions into backbenchers.

Even before the Sagawa Kyubin scandal, observers suggested that the size of the Takeshita faction made it unstable, likely to split eventually in a power struggle among second generation leaders. (That was the case with earlier large factions, like that of Prime Minister Sato.) To oversimplify, that scenario pitted second-tier leaders Ichiro Ozawa, Seiroku Kajiyama, Ryutaro Hashimoto, Keizo Obuchi, and Tsutomo Hata against each other. Now the troubles that have befallen the faction have led to its virtual breakup. The career of Takeshita himself, who has been Japan's most powerful politician for the last seven years, is in great jeopardy.

The Prospects for Reform

To restate Professor Kyogoku's proposition, indignation against the "upstarts"—those who profit from the unsatisfactory state of politics—does not seem to have reached the point at which public pressure is certain to force change. Similarly, while local and issue-oriented grassroots movements (women, consumers, and the environment) have taken on more life, they are not likely to be the precipitators of change in the short run.

Some kind of major event seems required to push Japanese politics out of entropy. To date, neither recession nor scandal has been sufficient. Some say, unhappily, that only the long-feared earthquake would surely force change. That "shock" (*shokku*) has become a prominent part of the political vocabulary (as in "the Nixon shocks") testifies to a sense of vulnerability to the unexpected. A seasoned Japanese observer sees latent anger among the citizenry, which could be triggered into activity by a prolonged recession, making the electorate quite volatile by the next Lower House election. Some spark—the economy, new revelations of scandal, or fear of political violence by the *yakuza* and the far Right—could motivate the public and the establishment to get serious about reform.

Effective leadership, in Japanese terms, has accompanied significant change. The parties could realign, but they need powerful leaders to bring it about. Similarly, a strong prime minister could revive electoral reform or override the bureaucracy to institute decentralization (a good place to start), but for the present a relatively powerless prime ministry seems more likely. The business community is edgy about political contributions, but the cost of politics may not hurt enough yet. A trillion yen per year is cited, but the figure may be twice as much—the squishy money is not likely to be included. On the other hand, as a businessman remarked, a recent calculation of business entertainment expenses (*kosaihi*) ran to 4 trillion yen. Still, one consequence of recession might be recognition by business that electoral reform is necessary to control the careening costs of politics.

Japanese business has demonstrated admirable innovation in economic matters but lacks political foresight. It is wedded to the notion of one-party rule, presumably because it promotes surface harmony in society. Still, in 1955 business played a crucial role in pushing conservatives to coalesce in the LDP. If business told the LDP it would withhold financing unless the electoral system were reformed, reform would come. Japan's businesses have long competed with each other. Lately, much of the business establishment has supported market liberalization, recognizing that Japan must buy from overseas competitors if it is to sell to them. It would be a short step to recognize that political competition would be good for business and for the nation. In the wake of Sagawa Kyubin, the head of the Keidanren has called for significant reform of the electoral system; whether that is serious or merely for show remains to be seen.

The most likely scenario is for not much to happen until either some event fires the Japanese or sub-surface currents in society rise to where they drive change forward, later in the decade. The third alternative is not a happy one: The triumph of a post-modern reverse course, based on Japanese exceptionalism, in which the remedy for the ills of democracy, a suspect import from abroad, is its further atrophy. Probably too much has changed for such a course, so that the tide of social and demographic change is likely to force reform by the end of the decade. But a worst-case scenario, involving a withering of democratic institutions in favor of a Japanified corporate state, cannot be dismissed out of hand, particularly should relations between the United States and Japan deteriorate significantly.

There is sentiment in Japan that argues that the nature of most Asian societies is so different from Western societies as to render American ideas about democracy irrelevant. For some, that idea is a mask for protecting Japanese business interests in places like Burma and Thailand, but it has gained currency. (The argument should be embarrassingly familiar: To justify expedient U.S. support for Latin American dictators, some Americans once argued that democracy was unsuitable for Latin societies.) So far Japanese who express that view tend to apply their logic to other Asian countries, and not to Japan. But if a clash of exceptionalisms between the U.S. and Japan should develop, theories about why political competition is unsuitable to the nature of the Japanese will reemerge.

That said, has the political crisis advanced the clock of reform? The answer, as this study goes to press, is "yes, but...." The tendency among elites is to temporize until the drama around Takeshita and his faction resolves itself. Much of what is heard from Nagata-cho (Japan's "inside the Beltway") is confined to tinkering with campaign finance or "reducing the power of the factions"—without specifying how. Except for reapportionment, discussed earlier, the Miyazawa cabinet has not taken a stand on reform. Opposition leaders appear equally paralyzed, unable to agree on a practical strategy, though Diet debate will help keep the Sagawa affair at a boil.

Away from Nagata-cho, the October 1992 polls told a different story. In *Mainichi*'s survey, 98 percent wanted Takeshita to explain links between the *yakuza* and politics and 75 percent wanted him to resign from the Diet, a call echoed by the prestigious *Nihon Keizai*. The *Sankei*'s survey showed 65 percent *not* supporting the Miyazawa cabinet, up from 50 percent the month before. Of those not supporting the cabinet, 48 percent cited political morality and reform (undefined), followed by the economy, as causes for their discontent. Takeshita's resignation, despite his repeated denials of direct involvement, appears imminent. While Prime Minister Miyazawa is distant from the scandal, the crisis could eventually bring down his government, precipitating Lower House elections.

New filings from the prosecution in the Sagawa case linked the affair to other LDP figures, including Keizo Obuchi, the formal replacement for Kanemaru as head of the Takeshita faction. More Diet members were alleged to have made approaches (or to have offered money) to quiet troublemakers. It is important to note that Obuchi and the others deny such involvement (one admitted to a phone call), but the allegations have raised more doubts.

A foreign observer surmises that the crisis is redrawing the political map along generational lines, stimulating grassroots politics. He may be correct. Rebels in the Takeshita faction are led by second generation figures Ichiro Ozawa and Tsutomu Hata, talking reform. Their followers are younger Diet members, while their more numerous antagonists are identified with the old system. In the provinces, young politicians of all political stripes, often with women in the forefront, backed "sense of the assembly" resolutions calling for Kanemaru to step down. (Japanese say that political and generational change in the United States helps the reform climate, much as the Watergate scandal made it easier to oust Tanaka.) In the opposition, restructuring is in the air. Governor Hosokawa's party, on the rise, crossed the old conservative-progressive boundary to converse with Rengo about cooperation. Others talk of a new, inclusive opposition. Some discuss change with LDP reformers. A common denominator is the presence of younger politicians.

The question is whether the body politic will be satisfied, as in the past, with resignations, modest changes in the conduct of elections, and, perhaps, a change of cabinet, or whether the public and the establishment will focus on the institutional causes of decay. The subsidiary but equally vital question is what form electoral reform might take. For example, controversy swirls around Ozawa, his ties to Kanemaru, and his previous insistence on undiluted single-member districts, to make the LDP the sole arbiter of constitutional change. The reformist credentials of Ozawa's ally, Hata, are secure, but it is not clear what formula the two now prefer. The reemergence of former Prime Minister Kaifu as a spokesman for reform may foreshadow the eventual outcome: a consensual formula, akin to those discussed earlier, to replace the old system without awakening fears of the "tyranny of the majority." If so, Japanese politics will likely undergo dramatic changes well before the end of the decade.

International Engagement

"*What does internationalization mean to Japanese? For most of us it's still a slogan.*"

—*a senior journalist, speaking of his countrymen*

Since two years ago, when the question at the top of this section was posed, there has been progress. It is not just public recognition that Japan has an obligation to provide economic assistance to less-fortunate countries or the quite recent public acceptance of a limited role in U.N. peacekeeping. For years, the Japanese version of the Peace Corps has been blessed with motivated volunteers. The talented young officials entering JICA (Japan's aid agency) choose the field because of a desire to make a contribution to the world. The patient work of private institutions like the Japan Council on International Exchange are bearing fruit. Educational and other exchanges are rife. A new element, reflective of changing society, is found in the rise of local grassroots groups dedicated to internationalization. Those go beyond the usual sister-city, sister-state relationships to volunteer-run groups dedicated to international endeavors ranging from reciprocal visits, educational programs for the community and volunteer help to developing countries, to international festivals in the provinces. The Ministry of Education program that places nearly 3,000 foreign language teachers, mostly from the U.S., in public schools, though constrained by archaic teaching methodology, is making an impact on attitudes towards the outside world in local communities, many of which welcome the teachers.

That said, Japan's engagement with the outside world is an unfinished story. More than a century has passed since the Black Ships ended Japan's seclusion. Notwithstanding all the wars, alliances, and changes in economy and political institutions, Japan still wrestles with how to relate to the world. The question is more domestic than international, involving Japan's sense of self. Japan could slide back toward the insularity that characterized most of its recorded history, or it could move firmly into a major constructive role in the twenty-first century community of nations.

Japan straddles its future in uncertain times. The equation is unstable and the decisions intensely political, hampered by what Japanese call "third-class politics," in contrast to a first-class economy. That characterization is unfair: There are many first-class people in politics. The better distinction is between a modern economy and a semi-feudal political culture just at a time when societal and global change appear to mandate greater political choice and more responsive politics.

Like it or not, the United States is part of that equation. The late prime minister Shigeru Yoshida supposedly said that when relations with the United States (and England) were good Japan went well. When they were not, Japan went badly. Geopolitical realities and a rather short historical record support his thesis. Presumably the quality of the relationship will help or hamper Japan as it grapples with internationalization.

There is a corollary, expressed by Japanese, to the effect that not only are Japan's security and economy linked to the United States, but that Japan's democratic institutions are contingent upon reasonably close ties. The opposite is almost certainly true. A Japan that repudiates democracy is a Japan that will repudiate its ties with the U.S. if the U.S. does not do it first. Most Japanese seem comfortable with democratic institutions. A distancing of relations, up to a point, would not cause political upheaval. Few Japanese want a break; some want more distance and less U.S. military presence, but not a rupture. The search for a "new nationalism," "Japanese de Gaullism," "autonomous security," has so far produced little more than reams of paper. The most plausible worst-case scenario is incremental, a withering of Japan's democratic institutions in a climate of public apathy and degradation of Japan-U.S. ties, each reinforcing the other.

Responsibility Sharing

It is hard for governments, among them our own, to make decisions, however necessary, that irritate entrenched interests.[6] In a time of political stagnation, it is hard to be innovative. We are asking for a greater Japanese commitment to international pursuits. That commitment requires that the public accept that internationalization has consequences for trading behavior and political engagement. Japan cannot expect to sell so much to the world and not buy more from it. Japan needs to say "yes" to foreign goods, to see reciprocal trade as a "win-win" scenario. Many understand that concept intellectually, but entrenched interests have held back measures to open markets every step of the way. Even incremental movement toward greater international participation requires decisions to change or alter budgets, laws, and policies. The record does not inspire confidence that change will come easily. If real political reform is not in the cards for the immediate future, forces in Japanese society that would take the country toward a more participatory role are not likely to find easy outlet for some time to come.

That is not to say that nothing will happen under a gradualist scenario. The peacekeeping bill, which would have been difficult to pass under any circumstances, reconciles the prohibition against war with support for a circumscribed role in U.N. efforts to keep the peace. In finally agreeing to amend the bill to meet the suggestions of two small parties, the Komeito and the DSP, the government showed common sense. The greatest praise should go to the Democratic Socialists, whose insistence on requiring Diet approval for each despatch of military personnel abroad assured the Japanese people and Japan's neighbors that the peoples' elected representatives will decide, rather than the bureaucracy.

Americans must press their views. But we need to search for ways to make it easier for Japan to respond. We would do well to abandon the lingo of "burdens," which appears to involve only those burdens we tell the Japanese to pick up. We need realistic rhetoric that recognizes Japan's right to share in decision making in return for taking on greater international responsibilities.

There is also a problem of style. Table pounding is in vogue among some Americans. In part it is a response to an equally dysfunctional Japanese negotiating style, and to legitimate frustration with the snail's pace of too many economic issues. But loud diplomacy is not effective, any more than the practice, attributed to British colonials, of speaking loudly in the belief that foreigners will understand English if one shouts. In Japan, to visibly blow one's stack is bad form. Worse, it is interpreted as a sign of weakness (the way many Japanese viewed Lee Iacocca's ire at Japan's automobile exports). It is not just a matter of common courtesy, but of a need for an effective negotiating style.[7]

The right style is important, but as a means to an end: coming to grips with major issues. Japanese gripe about "taxation without representation"—tasking Japan to write checks without much input into decisions. Fair enough. If we want to share responsibility, we have to share power, supporting a greater role for Japan in everything from international financial institutions to permanent membership in the U.N. Security Council. If changes are needed in U.N. peacekeeping arrangements—such as a permanent U.N. command structure to which countries could detail military personnel—to make it easier for Japan to participate in activities authorized by the U.N. Security Council, the U.S should support such change.

Gaiatsu

It is true, as people in Congress say, that foreign pressure (*gaiatsu*) has worked with Japan. But in advancing legitimate interests, a strategy that has pressure as its only lever appears subject to growing limitations. A hallmark of Japan's decision making has been to invite the U.S. to press for things that the leadership believes are in Japan's interests, and then say Japan was forced into them. Without political reform, the Japanese will recur to that sadomasochistic style of negotiations, with pain all around. The disadvantage, from an American perspective, is that Japanese who oppose what the U.S. suggests, however reasonable and however much in Japan's interest, get high ground by appealing to Japanese exceptionalism. Negotiations become a struggle, as the Tokyo press often describes them, between the United States, pushing Japan around, and a Japan that can never be understood by the foreigner.

To end *gaiatsu* at a stroke is impossible. Perhaps we can get more Japanese to see negotiations as a "win-win" scenario by frankly undertaking a campaign, aimed at public opinion, to explain why we believe Japanese agreement on specific issues is as much in Japan's interests as it is in ours. I was struck by the advice from Japanese of different walks of life that America needs to make its case more effectively to the public, and particularly to the Japanese media, which often foster a "poor little Japan" image. In particular, that applies to trade issues. The end, as desirable to Japanese as to Americans, would be to switch from *gaiatsu* to *naiatsu*—internal pressure from the Japanese themselves.

There is a further difficulty, which can only be remedied by the Japanese. The time is past when foreign experts could serve as the explainers of Japan, but in general Japanese remain unwilling to explain themselves. When the Japanese case is reasonable, as it fundamentally was in the Gulf war, hardly any Japanese will state publicly in plain language that "we are doing much more than you realize, and that is why we cannot do some things you ask."

Priorities

The United States cannot treat all issues as equally important, asking for action all at once. In the post–Cold War environment, the U.S. will need to articulate a sense of priority, often missing, in arraying its objectives. For example, trade and market openings will remain a top priority until the trade deficit comes down to a reasonable level, but which trade issues are most important? To which should we give priority? We need a visible strategy, one Japanese and Americans can readily understand.

This is not a paper about the U.S.-Japan relationship; such papers are not in short supply. But in the context of an inquiry into the consequences of political stagnation, there may be merit in linking this paper's judgments to a few suggestions about how the United States might focus its energies, at a time when Japan is likely to find it difficult to make decisions that depart from the status quo.

So many people from both sides of the Pacific have said in so many ways, without much happening, that the United States and Japan should articulate a new vision for a post–Cold War alliance, that the commonsense idea of a new agenda, responsive to the challenge of the coming century, risks becoming an endangered species. The Japanese establishment seems eager for a new framework. In the current climate it may be easier for a Japanese government to deal with macro issues, to set a course toward the future, than to deal with specifics. In any event, the inauguration of the Clinton administration will provide a chance to try again, perhaps the last opportunity before the two countries become chained to the Sisyphean task of dealing with everything at the micro-level.

The Japanese public also appears ready. The situation is reminiscent of 1960, when the "reverse course" and the contentious ratification of the Security Treaty precipitated malaise in Japan's politics and in relations with the United States. Then, a modern domestic strategy, the work of Ikeda and his advisors, coupled with a new and modern vision of interdependence between the two countries, the work of the Kennedy administration and Ambassador Edwin O. Reischauer in particular, reinvigorated ties by giving the Japanese public sensible reasons for alliance.

The task is greater now because publics on both sides of the Pacific must be persuaded. With the end of the Cold War, the need for reform, domestic and international, is palpable. Each will have to deal with its own problems; we cannot reform Japan's politics, nor they our educational system. Modernizing an alliance gone stale will require a practical agenda. A new framework would make it easier to deal with bilateral issues, including trade. It would also help the Japanese articulate a satisfactory role for themselves, to undertake what Japan's ambassador to the U.S., Takakazu Kuriyama, calls Japan's "third opening" to the modern world, after the first opening in the Meiji era and the second in the immediate postwar period.

A suggestion that Japan should raise international contributions to 3 percent of gross domestic product (GDP) bounces back and forth across the Pacific. Such contributions include those to self-defense, economic assistance to developing countries, the global environment, the U.N. system, and refugees, monies that currently run at about 1.7 percent of Japan's GDP. Of them, Japan's direct defense expenditures account for about 1 percent of GDP (plus military pension obligations). Economic assistance is about .03 percent—double that of the United States in per capita GDP terms but roughly the same in dollars, depending on the yen-dollar relationship.

In the future, Japanese defense costs will stabilize and are likely to decline over time—where is the threat, after all? Without a great convulsion, a Japanese commitment to expanding Japan's military is unlikely. In fact, major new Japanese military expenditures that go beyond current plans for modernization could *decrease* Japan's security by prompting an arms race in Asia, particularly with the Chinese. That equation seems well understood by most Japanese. But China itself could fall victim to the law of unintended consequences by stimulating Japanese security concerns through an excess of zeal in modernizing China's military. In a sensible scenario, however, new Japanese international expenditures would go to peaceful pursuits, including, it should be emphasized, U.N. peacekeeping.

The precedent exists. The Japanese contribution of $13 billion to the Gulf operation, not exactly small change, raised the Japanese contribution to international affairs to 2 percent of GDP. Were Japan to raise its international expenditures to 3 percent of GDP, it would level the playing field. U.S. international expenses, largely military, are headed down toward the 3 percent level from the 6–7 percent of GDP spent at the peak of the Cold War. Japan could decide to move that way, particularly if it involved a joint U.S.-Japanese strategy to promote development in the poor nations, secure the global environment, make the U.N.

more effective, and explore together the frontiers of science and medicine. Such a joint strategy is necessary in any event, at the heart of any new vision of cooperation.

The Pacific is an arena for post–Cold War cooperation, as Paul Volcker has argued, most recently in the book *Changing Fortunes*, written with Toyoo Gyooten. Described broadly, that effort would involve collaboration between the United States and Japan, working with other nations of the Pacific, including those of Latin America, to build a Pacific community of open trade and investment, the antidote to fears around the globe of trade blocs. The need for a "Pacific Community," which might include an eventual Pacific free trade area, was also argued in the final report of the Commission on U.S.-Japan Relations for the Twenty-first Century, a nonpartisan public interest group.

A second aspect of a Pacific dimension would involve taking the U.S.-Japan security relationship off automatic pilot and abandoning reticence about regional security, to take the lead in a Pacific dialogue. Such a dialogue would seek assurances that the region remains an area of peace providing a viable regional framework for continuing U.S.-Japan security cooperation in the post-containment era. Long-held concerns in Asia about Japan's future military posture and new concerns about the reach of China's military modernization, along with the uncertainties of an unnaturally divided Korean peninsula, will not be assuaged without dialogue. Such a dialogue might lead to eventual understandings about a Pacific regime for conventional arms limitations. There are various possibilities; the most likely venue would be a further evolution of APEC (Asia Pacific Economic Cooperation, the body that brings together the governments of the region).[8]

The two governments have been too cautious in exploring post-containment security arrangements for the Pacific, opposing even such modest ideas as a regional security and political dialogue, analogous but not identical to the the Conference on Security and Cooperation in Europe. The reasons for the caution range from the pedestrian ("Asia is not Europe") to a prevalence of a short-term calculus of interests in both countries—a belief that interests are most easily advanced in bilateral settings. Lately, the Japanese have become more adventurous, even calling for a Pacific summit that would deal with political as well as economic questions. In Tokyo, however, the proponents have not defined the objectives of regional dialogue, whether it is narrowly aimed at fortifying Japan's status as a regional power (which no one questions) or at working toward a broad Pacific structure of peace.

The American interest in pursuing a general security framework for the Pacific should be clear: the maintenance of the climate of peace that was originally conferred by the U.S.-Japan security relationship, but that needs to be redefined in the post–Cold War context. Without that climate of peace, the prospects dim for Pacific prosperity, prosperity in which Americans from the eastern seaboard to the West Coast have a major economic stake. If so, the United States will have to devote more resources to regional diplomacy in the Pacific than has been the case to date.

It is important, too, for Japan's Asian neighbors to understand that the U.S.-Japan alliance cannot be easily maintained in the framework that many seem to conceive for it, as primarily a check upon Japan. The U.S. cannot serve as ally and jailer all at once, and neither party could accept such a demeaning vision. Nor should they, when the alliance could become the centerpiece in a broader framework of Pacific security, a non-threatening assurance of stability.

Epilogue

In the aftermath of war, American power gave the Japanese (and Germans and Italians) new sets of democratic institutions. That those institutions have taken root is due to the temper of the people, however, rather than to American insistence. Indeed, some Americans (see William Sebald's *With MacArthur in Japan*), weighed down by the Cold War, shared the Japanese establishment's concern that General MacArthur's occupation had gone too far with democratic reforms, spurring fears of a communist takeover that appear quaint today. In Japan, intellectuals disenchanted with the ruling LDP inveighed against the distance between Japan's political parties and the desirable model, as they saw it, of West European parties with mass membership and a pronounced ideological stance, characteristics in short supply among Liberal Democrats.

None of those expedient critiques have much to do with what actually hobbles Japan's politics. In fact, the pragmatism of the LDP made it more responsive to the citizenry, more receptive to change in its early decades than it would have been as a European-style ideological party. Japan did not come near to communism, and Japan's prohibition against war making and against becoming a nuclear power was key to the successful containment of the Soviets and contributed enormously to stability in the Pacific after the Vietnam War.

The Japanese managed their democratic transition with considerable success. That their democratic institutions now face serious challenge should not surprise us; Americans, too, face troubles. Nothing is certain, but there is reason to believe that the Japanese will confront their political troubles; no one else can do it for them. The public needs to use its newfound voice to demand serious reform. That is not a prescription for American indifference, however. It is appropriate for Americans to remind allies that we are all in the democracy boat together, that we have as much right to be concerned about the health of their democracies as they have to be concerned about ours. We can join together in useful inquiry into how to make post–Cold War democratic institutions more responsive and effective. Such inquiry cannot be easily conducted by governments. The most promising avenue, avoiding vested interests and questions of sovereignty, lies in sponsorship by nongovernmental institutions.

Discussants of the Paper
Carnegie Endowment for International Peace

Morton Abramowitz, Carnegie Endowment

L. Desaix Anderson, Department of State

Daniel Bob, Office of Senator Roth

William L. Brooks,
Bureau of Intelligence & Research,
Department of State

Richard Bush, Subcommittee on
Asian & Pacific Affairs

James Clad, Carnegie Endowment

Rust M. Deming, Department of State

John Despres, Office of Senator Bradley

Michael Greene, Johns Hopkins School of Advanced
International Studies

Selig S. Harrison, Carnegie Endowment

David Hitchcock, U.S. Information Agency

Don Oberdorfer, The Washington Post

Marvin Ott, Senate Select Committee
on Intelligence

George Packard, Johns Hopkins School of Advanced
International Studies

Stanley Roth, Subcommittee on
Asian & Pacific Affairs

William Sherman, Reischauer Center,
Johns Hopkins University

Edson W. Spencer, Spencer Associates

Nathaniel Thayer, Reischauer Center,
Johns Hopkins University

Ezra Vogel, Harvard University

About The Author

Frank McNeil was a nonresident senior associate of the Carnegie Endowment for International Peace when he researched and wrote this essay. Previously, he had seen wide-ranging foreign service in Asia, Latin America, and southern Europe, with a total of ten years in Japan. When McNeil left the Foreign Service in 1987, the *Washington Post* and the *New York Times* described him as one of the most knowledgeable persons in the State Department about Japan. Three times deputy assistant secretary of state, he also served as U.S. ambassador to Costa Rica. In private life, he conducted a project on U.S.-Japan relations for the Council on Foreign Relations and most recently was executive director of the Commission on U.S.-Japan Relations for the Twenty-first Century, a nonpartisan public interest group of prominent Americans. He has written about democracy and foreign affairs, and his book, *War and Peace in Central America*, made the *New York Times* list of "notable books" of 1989. McNeil is working on a book about democracy in Japan for the Crown Publishing Group. He has recently taken up the directorship of the Strategic Studies Group at the Naval War College in Newport, Rhode Island.

Notes

1. The new conventional wisdom often treats Japan's democratic institutions as nonexistent or irrelevant. The lengthy index for the scare text, *The Coming War with Japan*, has no page references for democracy. That was no proofreading error; the potboiler omits discussion of Japan's political institutions from its plodding scenario (only Amelia Earhart is missing from a "history repeats itself" plot that includes repetition of the pre–World War II American embargo on Japanese oil). In their heyday America's strategic gurus were little better, advocating expedient change in Japan's constitution to serve Cold War military goals, without regard to the views of the Japanese people, who overwhelmingly opposed remilitarization.

2. The *Nihonjinron* (literally, the "theory of the Japanese") also survives in an apolitical way, in books about what makes Japan "different." Most cultures celebrate their identity or their search for it, and American exceptionalism is no less a fact than Japanese, but many foreign observers have remarked on what seems to them an unusual fascination of the Japanese public with books about what makes their country tick. It is in that context that the addiction of some Japanese to buying foreign books that are critical of their country should be understood. The more harsh the Western criticism, the more often it is cited as proof that Japanese exceptionalism is correct. There may be a strain of intellectual masochism at work, but whatever the sentimental state of the reader, many Japanese are avid purchasers of critical works by Western authors. If the authors are demonstrably ignorant, they may be excused because Japan is supposedly unknowable to outsiders. Of course Japanese, it should be understood, are by no means monolithic in their views. If criticism is close to the bone, some will frankly agree with it, but others will perceive the work from a conspiratorial perspective, as anti-Japanese, whether the label is warranted or not.

3. Western "revisionist" views of Japan—whatever the virtues of individual works—are as much a Japanese export as the concept of quality control was an American export to Japan. The frequent Japanese insistence on exceptionalism, on Japan's being so different from other societies as to be almost alien, is raw material for the new criticism. The latest theory, argued by some Japanese intellectuals and officials, has a clever twist: It is not Japan that is so exceptional but the United States. Our countries are different, of course, but that line of thought preserves the insular habit of focusing on differences with the West, to the exclusion of the commonalities of the human experience and the collective challenge of global change.

4. A change in the English translation of the Socialist party's name (but not in the Japanese), replacing "Socialist" with "Social Democratic," illustrates the party's taste for irrelevance. A Socialist office holder observed, "I can't explain it to English-speaking friends. My party's explanation—that years ago we were called Social Democrats in English—is not very persuasive. It certainly doesn't mean anything in Japan." (The ruling Spanish socialists provide instructive contrast: After Franco the PSOE—the Spanish Socialist Party—modernized its policies but never felt a need to change its name.)

5. Japanese criticize the workings of the Upper House because, among other reasons, the prefectural districts from which 152 of the 250 members are selected deviate considerably from "one person, one vote" in giving each prefecture from one to four seats. The intention of the framers—the formula is of Japanese inspiration, not a stipulation of the occupation, which preferred a unicameral legislature—was to provide regional representation. (The United States, it should be noted, displays an even more pronounced regional skew in the Senate.) The blue-ribbon commission that recommended sweeping revision of the Lower House electoral system chose not to make recommendations about the Upper House. The commission felt, as a member explained, that to recommend changes in the electoral system for both Houses at that time was more than the traffic would bear. Since the Lower House was predominant and the effects of its electoral system the most troubling, the commission concentrated on that body, leaving the Upper House to another day. Despite that commonsense approach, Prime Minister Kaifu could not push the reform through.

6. For many democratic countries, it is no longer just a matter of choosing among traditional options, but of deep-seated discontent, reflected in declining voter participation, as in Japan. It is not just in the U.S. where there is discontent and desire for change. French voters gave a disturbing 15 percent of the vote to Le Pen's racist political movement. John Majors held on to the prime ministry in Great Britain, but his government wallows in economic difficulty. Helmut Kohl is in trouble; local elections, unprecedented strikes, and neo-Nazi outrages show frustration with established parties and the costs of German reunification. No one knows how democracy will fare in Eastern Europe and what was once the Soviet Union. In the Third World—a different description is badly needed, and Barbara Ward's "poor nations" will do—the unvarnished optimism of the Reagan administration with respect to democracy has proven to be premature, as we see in Peru, Colombia, and even in Venezuela, where the unthinkable, a military coup, came perilously close to success.

7. Tracts about working in Japan tend to focus on how to get Japanese comfortable with Western counterparts. They properly stress courtesy, patience, and interchange in social settings before getting down to business. They do not, however, tell the reader much about how to disagree, which is a necessary part of genuine dialogue. Japanese do not expect us to stop being Americans and behave with Japanese indirection. Frankness is fine, expected, and admired in Americans. Displays of anger are not. To bizarre assertions such as "Japanese snow is different," the persuasive response is not anger, but ridicule. For genuine displeasure, icy politeness will suffice.

8. For a set of recommendations about the conduct of U.S.-Japan relations, see the *Final Report of the Commission on U.S.-Japan Relations for the Twenty-first Century*. For further discussion of the Pacific dimension, see the last chapter in the Volcker/Gyooten book, and *Preparing for a Pacific Century*, a report of the commission-sponsored conference in July of 1991, among American, Japanese, Korean, and Southeast Asian panelists and discussants. (The discussions were also carried on C-SPAN.)